THE RATIONAL PASSOVER HAGGADAH

THE
RATIONAL
PASSOVER
HAGGADAH

Dennis Prager

EDITED BY JOSEPH TELUSHKIN

THE ALPERSON EDITION

REGNERY
FAITH

ISBN: 978-1-68451-490-8

This paperback edition first printed 2023

Published in the United States by
Regnery Faith
An Imprint of Regnery Publishing
A Division of Salem Media Group
Washington, D.C.
www.SalemBooks.com

Manufactured in the United States of America

10 9 8 7 6 5 4 3 2 1

Books are available in quantity for promotional or premium use. For information on discounts and terms, please visit our website: www.Regnery.com.

To Joel Alperson, my friend who made
The Rational Passover Haggadah *and* The Rational Bible *possible,*
to his extraordinary wife, Conny, and to their children,
Hannah, Rachel, Aaron, and David, with whom I have a special bond

Contents

Introduction

Jews have celebrated Passover for more than three thousand years. It is probably the longest-observed ritual in the world.

I have written *The Rational Passover Haggadah* for many of the same reasons I wrote *The Rational Bible*, my commentary on the Torah. Biblical and other sacred texts need to be explained in a rational manner and made relevant. Like *The Rational Bible*, *The Rational Passover Haggadah* is meant for every type of Jew and for non-Jews.

But there is an additional reason, specific to *The Rational Passover Haggadah*. I have attended enough Seders to realize that even traditional Jews steeped in knowledge of Torah and Talmud, let alone more secular Jews and non-Jews, can use help in making their Seder discussions more interesting, deeper, and more accessible to every participant—as well as to those who may never attend a Seder.

Therefore, throughout *The Rational Passover Haggadah*, the reader will find topics marked "For Discussion." These topics, related to some part of the Haggadah, raise some great issue of life—again, of interest to the religious Jew, the non-religious Jew, and the non-Jew. Best of all, these topics give every participant at the Seder a reason to participate in the Seder, and will hopefully provoke young participants to speak up, or at least pay attention.

This Haggadah is not confined to Passover use, nor is it only for people who attend a Seder. It is intended for year-round use and for those who may never attend a Seder. As the reader can see from the table of contents, the essay topics and discussions are relevant to any time and to any individual. This Haggadah is intended to serve as a guide to life, to God, and to Judaism.

Acknowledgments

As was the case regarding *The Rational Bible*, *The Rational Passover Haggadah* would not have been written were it not for the efforts of Joel Alperson of Omaha, Nebraska. With the single exception of the actual writing of this Haggadah, he supervised every aspect of this project—just as he has with *The Rational Bible*. Most important, it was his cajoling that convinced me to write *The Rational Passover Haggadah*.

As with *The Rational Bible*, he convinced my lifelong friend, the eminent Jewish scholar and writer Rabbi Joseph Telushkin, to serve as editor of the project.

Joel Alperson and my wife, Susan Prager, who edits every word I write, also edited this work.

Aryeh Leifert, an American-born Israeli, served as an editor of the final manuscript. I benefited from his remarkable command of English grammar and from his ability to find typos even after four of us read every word aloud. His expertise in Jewish sources—he is a licensed Israeli tour guide and ordained rabbi—was also indispensable.

A special thank-you goes to Professor Leeor Gottlieb of the Department of Bible of Bar-Ilan University, the academic editor of *The Rational Bible*, for his scholarly contributions to this Haggadah.

Barney Brenner of Tucson, Arizona, is a final reader of the manuscript. I marvel at his gift for identifying errors as well as his biblical knowledge.

As with *The Rational Bible*, Holly Hickman of Dallas, Texas, a committed Christian and deep admirer of Judaism, raised important questions and provided indispensable insights.

Finally, I asked Avner Stein of Orlando, Florida, the final editor of my weekly column, to read the galleys of this Haggadah, and, as usual, his work was indispensable.

Dennis Prager
Los Angeles, California
September 1, 2021

THE RATIONAL PASSOVER HAGGADAH

The Passover Seder and the Haggadah

Given that the Passover Seder is the most widely observed Jewish ritual, most Jews—and an increasingly large number of non-Jews—are familiar with the Hebrew word "seder." However, few people know what the word means: it is the Hebrew word for "order." The modern Hebrew word for "OK"—*b'seder*—literally means "in order."

The name "order" was given to the Passover ritual meal because it is conducted in a set order. The Seder consists of fifteen steps written down in a book called the Haggadah (Hebrew for the "telling," because it tells the story of the Exodus from Egypt). Understand these steps and you will understand what the Rabbis wanted to achieve at the Passover Seder. "Rabbis" refers to the ancient rabbis who compiled the Talmud, the holiest Jewish work after the Hebrew Bible. The Talmud, finalized in about the year 500, is the size of a large encyclopedia. It is comprised of dozens of volumes containing philosophy, theology, legends, stories, and, most of all, arguments and discussions about how to carry out Jewish laws. The earliest date for the Haggadah is 170, but the finalized edition dates to approximately 750.

Why does the Haggadah exist? Because the Torah, the first five books of the Bible, commands Jews to tell the story of the Exodus during the holiday of Passover (see Exodus 13:8 and 13:14–15), but it does not specify how to do so. Post-biblical Jewish law did.

Were it not for the Seder and Haggadah, a person would fulfill the Torah commandment in any way he or she chose. Perhaps there would be a holiday meal with family and/or friends at which some people might discuss the Exodus; perhaps a rabbi or a group of Jewish laymen would discuss the Exodus at synagogue; or perhaps one would talk about the Exodus in a phone call with a friend or relative. All of these would theoretically fulfill the Torah law, but none would come close to being a Seder.

In addition, any Jew can fully celebrate the Seder with other Jews anywhere in the world. All Jews recite the same Haggadah and therefore have the same Seder.

Finally, while there is plenty of room for spontaneous discussion—as we will see, it is encouraged—the authors of the Haggadah wanted to ensure that Jews incorporate certain aspects of the Exodus story and the Passover holiday at the Seder.

It has worked well. Though Jews were exiled from their homeland for nearly 1,900 years, they not only retained their national identity—a unique achievement in human history

1

for a dispersed people—they also kept the story of their Exodus from Egypt alive. The Passover Haggadah and the Seder are what made that possible.

For Discussion
What Is More Important in Judaism—the Home or the Synagogue?

The central religious institution in Jewish life is not the synagogue. The synagogue, where Jews gather for communal prayer, is certainly important, but the central religious institution in Judaism is the home. The synagogue is essentially a religious adjunct to the home. The home is where the holidays—most important, the weekly Shabbat (Sabbath)—are celebrated. While many synagogues today conduct a Seder, the vast majority of Jews throughout Jewish history have observed the Seder in a home—either their own or that of a relative or friend.

That is why virtually no Jew celebrates the Seder alone. If Jews learn that some Jew has no home to go to for the Seder, it is likely he or she will be invited to someone's Seder. Within the context of Judaism, a Jew being alone on Seder night is particularly sad. After all, the purpose of the Seder and the Haggadah is to tell a story, and one needs others to whom to tell the story. Rosh Hashanah (the Jewish New Year) and Yom Kippur (the Day of Atonement) are the most important Jewish holidays (along with Shabbat)—hence they are referred to as the "High Holy Days"—and most Jews will have at least one High Holiday meal with other Jews. But it is the Seder meal that most Jews feel the greatest need to share with others.

Therefore, Jews should seriously consider inviting one or more individuals other than family and close friends to their Seder. There are undoubtedly Jews in your city who, for whatever reason, do not have family or friends with whom they are celebrating the Seder. No Jew should be alone on this night. At the same time, I also suggest inviting non-Jews to your Seder. For too long, Judaism has been hidden from the world. This has not done the Jews or the world any good.

THE SEDER

The Seder begins with the reading or chanting aloud of its fifteen steps—somewhat like starting a nonfiction book by reading aloud the chapter titles.

The Fifteen Steps of the Seder

1. **Kadesh:** Kadesh means "sanctify" or "consecrate." We begin the Seder by reciting a prayer of sanctification over wine.

2. **Urchatz:** A ritual washing of the hands. This is an act of purification, not a cleaning of the hands. Our hands are expected to already be clean before the ritual washing. The washing is a statement that one is about to engage in a holy act.

3. **Karpas:** We eat a vegetable such as parsley, celery, or potato (but not a bitter herb). This reminds those at the Seder that Passover falls in the spring, a time of rebirth and renewal.[1] Indeed, the Torah describes Passover as *chag he-aviv*, "the spring festival."

Nations that do not tell their story to each succeeding generation will eventually have no succeeding generation to whom to tell their story.

4. **Yachatz:** The word means "cut in half." There are three *matzot* (pieces of *matzah*, the unleavened bread of Passover) on the Seder leader's (and sometimes on other participants') plate. The leader (and any other participant who wishes) breaks the middle *matzah* in half. The larger of the two pieces is then set aside to be consumed as the final item eaten at the Seder.

5. **Magid:** The word means "tell." It is the same word as the root of the word *Haggadah*, "the telling"—of the story of the Exodus. This is the longest and most important part of the Seder. Telling the story is the purpose of the Haggadah and, for that matter, of Passover.

Nations that do not tell their story to each succeeding generation will eventually have no succeeding generation to whom to tell their story. More on this in the Magid section.

6. **Rachtzah:** This is the second washing of the hands (*rachtzah* is from the same word as *urchatz*). The first, which had no accompanying blessing, is unique to the Passover Seder. This second washing is accompanied by a blessing—the same blessing recited before all other meals in Judaism.

7. **Motzi:** The word means "brings forth," the Hebrew word contained in the traditional blessing recited when eating bread: *Baruch ata Adonai, Eloheinu melech ha-olam, ha-motzi lechem min ha-aretz* (Blessed are You, Lord, King of the universe, Who brings forth bread from the earth). The reason the blessing over bread is recited is that *matzah* is bread, but it is *unleavened* bread.

8. **Matzah:** This is the unique blessing for the first eating of *matzah* on Passover. Eating *matzah* on Passover is so important that the Torah refers to Passover as Chag HaMatzot, the "Holiday of *Matzot*."

9. **Maror:** The word means "bitter." This is the bitter herb (raw horseradish is commonly used), eaten to remind us of the bitterness of slavery.

10. **Korech:** This alludes to a "sandwich" that combines the bitter herb and the sweet *haroset* (a paste usually comprised of apples, nuts, and cinnamon among other ingredients) between pieces of *matzah*.

11. **Shulchan Orech:** The words literally mean "Set Table," and signify the luxuriant Passover meal.

12. **Tzafun:** The word means "hidden." The meal ends with the eating of the hidden *matzah* which was broken at the beginning of the Seder. This piece of *matzah*—about which more will be said later—is known as the *afikoman*, derived from the Greek word for dessert. Subsequent to the *afikoman*, the Jewish practice is not to eat anything, with the exception of drinking the third and fourth cups of wine (or grape juice, if a substitute for wine is necessary—see pages 10–11 for an explanation of the four cups of wine). Considering how delicious the meal and the desserts were, the *afikoman* is admittedly a letdown. However, the Rabbis were more interested in meaning than in cuisine.

13. **Barech:** The word means "bless" and refers to the Birkat HaMazon, the Grace after Meals, a series of prayers thanking God for the food and much else.

14. **Hallel:** The word means "praise" and is the root of the well-known Hebrew word "Hallelujah." Some psalms from the Book of Psalms are recited.

15. **Nirtzah:** The word means "acceptance." This is the Seder's completion, when we pray that "just as we were able to carry out the Seder's order this year, so may we be able to carry it out again."

For Discussion
Why Are Rituals Important, Even Vital?

As noted in the introduction, Jews have celebrated Passover for thousands of years. It is most likely the longest-observed ritual in the world, a testament to the power of ritual to perpetuate gratitude and national identity, both of which rely on memory.

Memory, in turn, relies on ritual. Human beings find perpetuating gratitude very difficult. Unless people make a deliberate effort, the good that another has done for them is usually forgotten quickly. Remembering hurtful things comes far more naturally to people than remembering the good things done to them. That Jews have been grateful to God for the Exodus for over three thousand years is solely due to their observance of Passover, which is all the more remarkable in light of all the terrible suffering Jews have since experienced.

The need for ritual is just as true in secular life. Using America as an example, the holidays with the most observed rituals—Thanksgiving and Christmas—remain widely observed. On the other hand, holidays during which few or no rituals are observed—Presidents' Day, for example—remain on the calendar, but are observed only as vacation days and are essentially devoid of meaning.

> *Remembering hurtful things comes far more naturally to people than remembering the good things done to them.*

There is also a proof within Jewish life of the need for ritual. The reason Passover is the best-known and most widely celebrated of the three festivals is thanks to its Passover Seder ritual. The next best-known Torah festival (though not nearly as widely celebrated) is Sukkot (tabernacles), also because of its rituals of building a *sukkah* (booth) for the holiday (see Deuteronomy 16:13–15), gathering with friends and family in the *sukkah* for meals, and daily blessings over a *lulav* (palm frond) and *etrog* (citron), along with myrtle and willow. The least well-known of the three festivals among Jews is Shavuot (Pentecost)—precisely because it is essentially devoid of specific rituals (though many Jews engage in the ritual of studying the Torah much of, or even the entire, night).

A post-Torah holiday, Chanukah, commemorating an event that occurred about 1,100 years after the Exodus, is widely observed precisely because of the ritual of lighting an additional candle each night of the holiday's eight days. Chanukah would not be nearly as widely observed if not for the holiday's candle-lighting ritual (and, in the West, because of its proximity to Christmas).

קדש
KADESH
(The Kiddush)

In keeping with the central theme of the holiday, the Passover Kiddush—the blessing over the wine—speaks of "the feast of *Matzot*, the season of our freedom . . . in memory of the Exodus from Egypt."

The blessing over the wine itself—*Blessed are You, Lord our God, Who has created the fruit of the vine*—is but one sentence, placed between the two large paragraphs of the Kiddush.

The Torah's command that the Jew be happy is what shaped my understanding of happiness—that it is both a choice and a moral obligation.

Another one-sentence blessing is appended at the end of the Kiddush: *Blessed are You . . . Who has kept us alive, sustained us, and brought us to this time.* This blessing, known as the *shehecheyanu*, is said on holidays and other happy occasions. It is intended to ensure that people express gratitude for the good things—even minor good things—in their lives. It is, therefore, not only recited at the start of Jewish holidays, but when tasting a fruit for the first time in any given season, when putting on new clothes, or when moving into a new house.

Regarding the joyousness of the holiday, there are actually laws in the Torah that command the Jew "to be happy" on the festivals—specifically Shavuot and Sukkot (Deuteronomy 16:11, 13–16). Interestingly, the Torah does not command happiness on the third of the three festivals, Passover. On Passover, the Torah assumes the believing Jew will be happy, given that the holiday is about escaping slavery. The emotion the Torah and later Judaism seek to evoke on Passover is gratitude (which, as it happens, is the primary creator of happiness). In effect, the gratitude inculcated by Passover makes the happiness of the other two festivals possible.

The Torah's command that the Jew be happy is what shaped my understanding of happiness—that it is both a choice and a moral obligation. Most people think happiness is a feeling or emotion that one either has or doesn't have at any given moment. Judaism made me realize that happiness is largely a choice. As the American president Abraham Lincoln, who suffered terrible emotional pain throughout his life, put it, "People are about as happy as they make up their minds to be."

So even if you are in a bad mood as Passover begins—or, for that matter, at any time in life—you owe it to all those around you to act as happy as you can (or, at the very least, not to inflict your bad mood on them). That is another significant insight Judaism has contributed: feelings should not dictate behavior, and behavior shapes feelings.

Pour the first cup. The *matzahs* remain covered. The Kiddush ("Sanctification") over the wine is usually recited by the leader of the Seder. At many Seders, others recite the Kiddush after the leader does. Lift the cup and recite/sing the Kiddush in Hebrew or in whatever language(s) the participants understand best. Outside of Israel, many Seder participants do not know Hebrew; therefore the most important sections of the Haggadah should be recited in the participants' native language. For example, the leader might chant the Kiddush in Hebrew and then ask another participant to recite the Kiddush in English.

If Passover begins on a Friday night (Shabbat), the Kiddush begins with the first paragraph of the weekly Shabbat Kiddush. It consists entirely of the Torah's description of God making Shabbat, the culmination of Creation (Genesis 1:31–2:3).

> (וַיְהִי-עֶרֶב וַיְהִי-בֹקֶר) יוֹם הַשִּׁשִּׁי. וַיְכֻלּוּ הַשָּׁמַיִם וְהָאָרֶץ וְכָל-צְבָאָם. וַיְכַל
> אֱלֹהִים בַּיּוֹם הַשְּׁבִיעִי מְלַאכְתּוֹ אֲשֶׁר עָשָׂה וַיִּשְׁבֹּת בַּיּוֹם הַשְּׁבִיעִי מִכָּל מְלַאכְתּוֹ
> אֲשֶׁר עָשָׂה. וַיְבָרֶךְ אֱלֹהִים אֶת יוֹם הַשְּׁבִיעִי וַיְקַדֵּשׁ אוֹתוֹ כִּי בוֹ שָׁבַת מִכָּל-
> מְלַאכְתּוֹ אֲשֶׁר בָּרָא אֱלֹהִים לַעֲשׂוֹת.

(And there was evening, and there was morning), the sixth day. And the heaven and the earth were finished, and all their host. And on the seventh day God finished His work which He had done; and He rested on the seventh day from all His work which He had done. And God blessed the seventh day, and sanctified it; because He rested on it from all the work of creation that He had done.

If the Seder takes place on any night other than Shabbat, the Kiddush begins with the following (the words in brackets are added on Friday night):

בָּרוּךְ אַתָּה ה', אֱלֹהֵינוּ מֶלֶךְ הָעוֹלָם בּוֹרֵא פְּרִי הַגָּפֶן.

Blessed are You, Lord our God, King of the universe, Who creates the fruit of the vine.

(Baruch ata Adonai, Eloheinu melech ha'olam bo'rei pri ha'gafen.)

בָּרוּךְ אַתָּה ה', אֱלֹהֵינוּ מֶלֶךְ הָעוֹלָם אֲשֶׁר בָּחַר בָּנוּ מִכָּל־עָם וְרוֹמְמָנוּ מִכָּל־לָשׁוֹן
וְקִדְּשָׁנוּ בְּמִצְוֹתָיו. וַתִּתֶּן לָנוּ ה' אֱלֹהֵינוּ בְּאַהֲבָה (שַׁבָּתוֹת לִמְנוּחָה וּ) מוֹעֲדִים
לְשִׂמְחָה, חַגִּים וּזְמַנִּים לְשָׂשׂוֹן,(אֶת יוֹם הַשַּׁבָּת הַזֶּה וְ) אֶת יוֹם חַג הַמַּצּוֹת הַזֶּה
זְמַן חֵרוּתֵנוּ (בְּאַהֲבָה) מִקְרָא קֹדֶשׁ זֵכֶר לִיצִיאַת מִצְרָיִם. כִּי בָנוּ בָחַרְתָּ וְאוֹתָנוּ
קִדַּשְׁתָּ מִכָּל הָעַמִּים (וְשַׁבָּת וּ)מוֹעֲדֵי קָדְשֶׁךָ (בְּאַהֲבָה וּבְרָצוֹן) בְּשִׂמְחָה וּבְשָׂשׂוֹן
הִנְחַלְתָּנוּ .בָּרוּךְ אַתָּה ה', מְקַדֵּשׁ (הַשַּׁבָּת וְ) יִשְׂרָאֵל וְהַזְּמַנִּים.

*Blessed are You, Lord our God, King of the universe, Who has chosen us from all nations
and has raised us above all tongues and has sanctified us with His commandments. And
You have given us, Lord our God [Sabbaths for rest], appointed times for happiness,
holidays and special times for joy, [this Sabbath day, and] this Festival of Matzot, our
season of freedom [in love], a holy convocation in memory of the Exodus from Egypt.
For You have chosen us and sanctified us above all peoples. In Your gracious love, You
granted us Your [holy Sabbath, and] special times for happiness and joy. Blessed are You,
O Lord, Who sanctifies [the Sabbath,] Israel, and the appointed times.*

If the Seder falls on a Saturday night, the following is added. It is the traditional Havdalah ("Separation") prayer said at the end of Shabbat and all other Torah holidays, marking the separation of the special time from the rest of time.

בָּרוּךְ אַתָּה ה', אֱלֹהֵינוּ מֶלֶךְ הָעוֹלָם, בּוֹרֵא מְאוֹרֵי הָאֵשׁ. בָּרוּךְ אַתָּה ה', אֱלֹהֵינוּ
מֶלֶךְ הָעוֹלָם הַמַּבְדִּיל בֵּין קֹדֶשׁ לְחֹל, בֵּין אוֹר לְחֹשֶׁךְ, בֵּין יִשְׂרָאֵל לָעַמִּים, בֵּין
יוֹם הַשְּׁבִיעִי לְשֵׁשֶׁת יְמֵי הַמַּעֲשֶׂה. בֵּין קְדֻשַּׁת שַׁבָּת לִקְדֻשַּׁת יוֹם טוֹב הִבְדַּלְתָּ,
וְאֶת־יוֹם הַשְּׁבִיעִי מִשֵּׁשֶׁת יְמֵי הַמַּעֲשֶׂה קִדַּשְׁתָּ. הִבְדַּלְתָּ וְקִדַּשְׁתָּ אֶת־עַמְּךָ
יִשְׂרָאֵל בִּקְדֻשָּׁתֶךָ.

*Blessed are You, Lord our God, King of the universe, Who creates the lights of fire.
Blessed are You, Lord our God, King of the universe, Who distinguishes between the
holy and the profane, between light and darkness, between Israel and the nations,*

between the seventh day and the six working days. You have distinguished between the holiness of the Sabbath and the holiness of the Festival, and You have sanctified the seventh day above the six working days. You have distinguished and sanctified Your people Israel with Your holiness.

The Havdalah prayer normally ends with the words "between the holy and the secular," but when the Seder is on a Saturday night, Shabbat is not followed by the secular Sunday but by another holy day: Passover. Therefore, the Havdalah ends with the words "between the holy and the holy."

בָּרוּךְ אַתָּה ה', הַמַּבְדִיל בֵּין קֹדֶשׁ לְקֹדֶשׁ.

Blessed are You, O Lord, Who distinguishes between the holy and the holy.

בָּרוּךְ אַתָּה ה', אֱלֹהֵינוּ מֶלֶךְ הָעוֹלָם, שֶׁהֶחֱיָנוּ וְקִיְּמָנוּ וְהִגִּיעָנוּ לַזְּמַן הַזֶּה.

Blessed are You, Lord our God, King of the universe, Who has granted us life and sustenance and permitted us to reach this season.

For Discussion
Why Are Distinctions at the Heart of Judaism?

As noted, every Shabbat and Jewish holy day ends with the Havdalah prayer. Havdalah means "separation," and separation, or distinction, is one of the most important concepts in the Torah and Judaism. One could say the Torah is based on distinctions.

God-made distinctions constitute divine order. The first chapter of Genesis is as much about God making order as it is about God creating. The state of the universe before divine order was, as described in the second verse of the Torah, chaos (*tohu vavohu*). God is the Maker of Order and Distinctions. In Genesis 1, God distinguishes between:

Light and dark
Day and night
Land and water
Good and evil
Human and animal

Man and woman
God and man
God and nature

Later, the Torah makes distinctions between:

Holy and profane
Parent and child
Life and death

Preserving God's order and distinctions is one of man's primary tasks. The battle for higher civilization may be characterized as the battle between biblical distinctions and the desire of many "post-modern" individuals to eradicate many of those distinctions. As Western society abandons the Bible and the God of the Bible, it is abandoning these distinctions. The Havdalah prayer reminds the Jew how important distinctions are.

For Discussion
Why Does Judaism Allow, Even Call for, Consuming Wine?

The Seder begins, as do all Jewish holy day meals, with a blessing over wine. In Judaism, alcohol consumption has always been allowed and even mandated on holy days. The name of the prayer over the wine is Kiddush, which is another form of the Hebrew word for "holy," *kadosh*. The Jew drinks on a holy day and, through the Kiddush, renders the act of drinking holy. The purpose of Jewish drinking is to celebrate the holidays with added joy. As Psalm 104:15 puts it, "Wine gladdens the heart." Of course, an alcoholic should not drink wine at the Seder or at any other time; at the Seder, he or she should substitute grape juice. Similarly, if wine, particularly the four cups mandated for the Seder, causes you to be sleepy or gives you a headache, you should either not drink four full cups or consider drinking grape juice. The purpose of the four cups of wine is to increase your joy of the occasion, not diminish it.

The Jewish attitude toward wine can be summarized by a well-known Hebrew phrase: "respect it and suspect it" (*kabdayhu ve'chashdayhu*). Alcohol can enable or even lead to evils such as child and spousal abuse, rape, and murder, not to mention out-of-control anger. It is impossible to measure the amount of human suffering caused by alcohol. Ask anyone who has been raised by an alcoholic parent or who has an alcoholic spouse or child, or anyone who has lost a loved one to a drunk driver.

It is therefore understandable that some religions—such as Islam, Mormonism (Latter-Day Saints), and some Christian denominations—prohibit consumption of alcohol. The Jewish view is that the desire for alcohol, like most desires, should not be suppressed, but channeled into decent and holy ends. This attitude largely worked well for Jews, who historically had low rates of alcoholism. But as Jews began drinking for pleasure rather than to celebrate holy days, their alcoholism rates increased.

While Judaism mandates alcohol on holy days, and while the Torah does not forbid it, when the Torah mentions wine, it almost always associates it with negative events. One example is the story of Noah and his son (Genesis 9:20–25), who, after Noah gets drunk, sexually humiliates (or worse) his father. Another negative story concerning wine appears in Genesis 19:30–36. Lot's daughters, fearing no men are left alive after the destruction of Sodom and Gomorrah, get their father drunk on wine and sleep with him to produce offspring. And Leviticus 10:9 legislates with the most severe threat that priests must abstain from any consumption of wine while performing their work in the Sanctuary.

Nevertheless, the Rabbis decreed, "Even the poorest man in Israel . . . shall have no fewer than four cups of wine, even [if the wine comes] from the communal coffer."[2] This prescription applies to women as well and is unique in Judaism—because Passover and the Seder are unique. On this night, more than any other, the Jew, no matter how poor or troubled, is to feel prosperous and free.

The four cups represent the four expressions of deliverance promised by God in Exodus 6:6–7:

"I will bring out."
"I will deliver."
"I will redeem."
"I will take."

ורחץ
URCHATZ
(And Wash)

Wash your hands but do not say the traditional blessing "on the washing of the hands" (*al netilat yadayim*). Pour water over your hands. At all other meals of the year the ritual washing of one's hands is done at a sink, but not tonight. This special washing is done at the Seder table. Someone brings a pitcher of water and a bowl to each of the Seder participants, and each person pours water twice over the right hand and then twice over the left hand.

As previously noted, the purpose of this unique washing is not to clean one's hands, which should be clean before coming to the Seder table, but, among many other reasons offered by the Rabbis, to make it apparent that one is embarking on a particularly holy meal.

כרפס
KARPAS
(Greens)

Take a small amount of the greens or other vegetable (less than the size of an olive, according to tradition), dip it into the salt water, and say the blessing below, having in mind that this blessing will also cover the bitter herbs to be eaten later. Generally, parsley, celery, or potato is used, and almost any other vegetable is permitted. What is not permitted is any vegetable that can be used as a bitter herb (horseradish, for example)—because the eating of a bitter herb is a separate law to be fulfilled later in the Seder. The vegetable is dipped in salt water (reminiscent of the tears of slaves), and one then recites the blessing over vegetables:

בָּרוּךְ אַתָּה ה', אֱלֹהֵינוּ מֶלֶךְ הָעוֹלָם, בּוֹרֵא פְּרִי הָאֲדָמָה.

Blessed are You, Lord our God, King of the universe, Who creates the fruit of the earth.

יחץ

YACHATZ
(Break the *Afikoman* in Half)

The head of the household, and anyone else who has a plate with three *matzot*, breaks the middle *matzah* in two. The smaller half is placed between the two other *matzot*. The larger piece is wrapped and hidden somewhere in the vicinity of the Seder table. This piece of *matzah* will be used for the *afikoman*, the final food eaten at the Seder meal.

As we will see, some of the Seder's most important ceremonies are performed by children. One of the primary purposes, if not the primary purpose, of the Seder is to teach children—the next generation of Jews—about the Exodus, the most important event in their history.

In order to help keep children awake as long as possible—ideally at least until the *afikoman* is eaten at the end of the meal (which is not the conclusion of the Seder), a playful tradition developed long ago. The Seder leader "hides" the *afikoman* and the children try to find it. When they do (they always do), they "steal" it, and hide it themselves. Since, as noted, the Seder cannot proceed after the meal until the *afikoman* is eaten, one or more of the children then ask for a ransom in return for the *afikoman*.

A typical scenario might go like this: As the meal draws to an end, the Seder leader prepares to distribute the *afikoman* by retrieving it from its hiding place but "discovers" that it has disappeared! He announces, "I can't find the *afikoman*," at which point one or more of the children proudly declare, "I took it, and I will return it for a reward." The leader then says, "What would you like?" Then the child might name some toy or game or even something as expensive as a bicycle. I received the finest material gifts of my teenage years not for my birthday or for Chanukah, but for returning the *afikoman* at the Passover Seder.

One year, my grandfather, the nominal leader of the Seders of my youth, gave me a shortwave radio—a radio capable of tuning into radio stations throughout the world. That gift was one of the most important I ever received. It changed my life by opening my mind to the world. I listened to it virtually every night (except for Shabbat) of my high school and college years. Another year, he gave me a portable typewriter, which prompted me to start writing. So I have the fondest memories of "stealing" the *afikoman*, not to mention of my grandfather.

Of course, the gifts need not be extravagant. But the *afikoman* ritual serves its primary purpose—keeping the children awake. It also gives the children a sense of importance at the Seder in that the meal's completion depends on their returning the *afikoman*. And it is fun for children to engage in adult-like behavior by negotiating with their parents or grandparents.

Some moralists object to this whole enterprise, arguing that it encourages children to steal. Speaking personally, I can only express sadness for children whose parents refuse to play this game; humorless parents can be a challenge. Children are no more likely to become thieves because they stole the *afikoman* than become pirates because they dressed up as one on Purim.

מגיד
MAGID
(Telling—the Exodus Story)

The leader uncovers the *matzot*, raises the Seder plate, and says out loud:

הָא לַחְמָא עַנְיָא דִּי אֲכָלוּ אַבְהָתָנָא בְּאַרְעָא דְמִצְרָיִם. כָּל דִּכְפִין יֵיתֵי וְיֵיכֻל,
כָּל דִּצְרִיךְ יֵיתֵי וְיִפְסַח. הָשַּׁתָּא הָכָא, לְשָׁנָה הַבָּאָה בְּאַרְעָא דְיִשְׂרָאֵל. הָשַּׁתָּא
עַבְדֵי, לְשָׁנָה הַבָּאָה בְּנֵי חוֹרִין.

This is the bread of affliction that our ancestors ate in the land of Egypt. Anyone who is hungry should come and eat, anyone who is in need should come and partake of the Pesach rituals. Now we are here, next year we will be in the land of Israel; this year we are slaves, next year may we be free people.

The Magid section begins with a passage in Aramaic, the language Jews spoke at the beginning of the Common Era.

People understandably assume "hungry" and "in need" are synonyms, used here to reinforce the importance of providing for the poor. But they are not necessarily synonymous.

It might have been the intention of the author of this prayer to communicate that poor people are not necessarily needy (other than materially) and that many needy people are not necessarily poor. We are to care for both on Passover.

With regard to the hungry, Passover, with its feast-like meal, requires Jews to make sure that food is made available for the holiday for everyone. For this reason, Jewish communities have always had *maot chittin* funds, money specifically earmarked to ensure people have the means to celebrate Passover with a certain measure of luxury.

The "needy" refers to people in need of things in addition to, or other than, food. Perhaps the most common example is the need for companionship. In speaking with tens of thousands of people over nearly forty years—by phone on my radio show and in person—I was shocked to learn that vast numbers of people are lonely. Vast numbers of people do

16

not have close friends, and an even greater number of people have no community. Among the many prices people pay for having abandoned religion is a lack of community. There are few, if any, secular communities that have replaced religious communities.

Natan Sharansky, the long-imprisoned hero of the Soviet Jewry movement that began in the 1960s to enable Soviet Jews to emigrate from the Soviet Union, wrote about his experience. Several decades after leaving Russia for Israel, where he became a major political figure, Sharansky wrote a memoir, *Never Alone*, whose theme, reflected in the book's title, was that by belonging to the Jewish people, even in solitary confinement, he never felt alone. On Passover, no Jew should be alone. That is what this prayer calls on us to provide: food and community.

The Four Questions

Pour a second cup of wine. Then, a child, usually the youngest who can speak, asks the famous "Four Questions" of the Passover Seder:

מַה נִּשְׁתַּנָּה הַלַּיְלָה הַזֶּה מִכָּל הַלֵּילוֹת?

שֶׁבְּכָל הַלֵּילוֹת אָנוּ אוֹכְלִין חָמֵץ וּמַצָּה, הַלַּיְלָה הַזֶּה – כֻּלּוֹ מַצָּה.

שֶׁבְּכָל הַלֵּילוֹת אָנוּ אוֹכְלִין שְׁאָר יְרָקוֹת – הַלַּיְלָה הַזֶּה (כֻּלּוֹ) מָרוֹר.

שֶׁבְּכָל הַלֵּילוֹת אֵין אָנוּ מַטְבִּילִין אֲפִילוּ פַּעַם אֶחָת – הַלַּיְלָה הַזֶּה שְׁתֵּי פְעָמִים. שֶׁבְּכָל הַלֵּילוֹת אָנוּ אוֹכְלִין בֵּין יוֹשְׁבִין וּבֵין מְסֻבִּין – הַלַּיְלָה הַזֶּה כֻּלָּנוּ מְסֻבִּין.

Why is this night different from all other nights?

1. On all other nights we eat chametz *and* matzah; *this night, only* matzah.

2. On all other nights we eat other vegetables; tonight, [only] maror.

3. On all other nights, we do not dip [our food] even one time; tonight, [we dip it] twice.

4. On all other nights, we eat either sitting or reclining; tonight, we all recline.

The Four Questions, marking the unofficial opening of the Seder, accomplish at least three important goals.

First, they establish that the Seder is next-generation oriented. Teaching the next generation what the previous generation stands for and seeks to perpetuate is the only way a religion or a nation can survive. It is certainly the reason Jews are the longest living continuous culture. It is also why, at the time of this writing, the American and Western value systems are in danger of not being perpetuated. Depending on the Western country, since either World War I, World War II, or the Vietnam War, many members of the adult generation failed to teach the next generation American and Western values.

Second, standing up and asking these questions gives the Jewish child a chance to "perform" publicly—usually for the first time in his or her life. The self-confidence this imbues in most children is priceless. And its association with a Jewish experience can be life-shaping.

Third, these questions teach the Jewish child that the path to learning is through asking questions.

Questions played a critical role in Jewish life from the very beginning, and in the Bible they are often directed to God. Abraham, the first Jew, challenged God: "Shall not the judge of all the earth act justly?" (Genesis 18:25). The Psalmist similarly challenged God: "Why do You hide Your face, ignoring our afflictions and distress?" (Psalms 44:25). And the prophet Jeremiah posed a question that even pious believers still ask: "Why does the way of the wicked prosper?" (Jeremiah 12:1).

Unlike these theological questions, the Four Questions of the Haggadah are directed not at God, but at one's parents. Given the central importance of the Four Questions, however, the ironic fact is that few fathers or mothers actually answer them.

This is exemplified by an old Jewish joke:

At the Seder, the family expectantly waits for young Judah to recite these questions as he has done for the past two years. But the boy remains seated. His parents motion for Judah to stand, but he remains seated. Finally, they tell him to rise and recite the Four Questions.

"I won't do it," the boy says.

The parents and all the guests are shocked.

"Why not?"

"Every year I ask the Four Questions," the boy responds, "and Papa never answers them. It's clear he doesn't know the answers. So I'm not going to ask again. It's not nice for Papa."

The truth is there are plenty of papas and mamas who don't know the answers. Here, then, are the Four Questions and at least one papa's answers:

For Discussion
Suggested Responses to the Four Questions

First Question: "Why is it that on all other nights we eat both leavened bread and also *matzah*, but on this night we eat only *matzah*?"

Answer: When the Jews fled Egypt, they left on such short notice they had no time to wait for the bread to rise, so they took the bread from the ovens while it was still flat. In addition, eating *matzah* makes the point that it is better to eat a "poor man's bread" and be free than to eat tasty soft bread but live in slavery. This point alone is worth the whole holiday.

Freedom is a value, not an innate human desire. Many people prefer tasty food to liberty (the Jews in the desert, for example), and most people prefer to be taken care of than to be free.

If liberty were an innate yearning—as much as or more than being taken care of—there would be many more free societies than there are. France gave America the Statue of Liberty because America, for all its history until the present time, has been the freest country in the world. Why has it been? Because America was founded to be free. That is why its iconic symbol is the Liberty Bell, on which, it should be noted at the Seder, is inscribed one verse—a verse from the Torah: "Proclaim liberty throughout all the land unto all the inhabitants thereof" (Leviticus 25:10). Of course, America did not live up to its belief in liberty with regard to blacks. Half the country practiced slavery, and slavery is the opposite of liberty. But slavery was practiced in every nation and among every ethnic and racial group in history. What has rendered America unique is not its having practiced slavery, but that it became the freest country in the world.

> *Freedom is a value, not an innate human desire. Most people prefer to be taken care of than to be free.*

Second Question: "Why is it that on other nights we eat all kinds of herbs, but on this night we eat only bitter herbs?"

Answer: We eat the *maror*, the bitter herb, to remind us of the bitterness of the slavery our ancestors endured in Egypt.

Third Question: "Why is it that on other nights we don't even dip our herbs once, but on this night we dip them twice?

Answer: The two dippings refer to the dipping early in the Seder of the green vegetable into salt water and the dipping later in the Seder of the bitter herb into the *haroset*, the sweet mixture of nuts, wine, and apples or other fruits. The salt water in which the vegetable is dipped symbolizes the tears shed by the oppressed slaves. *Haroset* appears in the Mishnah, meaning that it was eaten at the Seder at least two thousand years ago. Yet its precise reason for being has been lost. Some say it represents the mortar the Israelite slaves used when laying bricks. Some say it has the opposite purpose: an attempt to lessen the bitterness of the *maror*. Still others, according to Leeor Gottlieb, professor of Bible at Israel's Bar-Ilan University, "found in it a symbolic significance, meant to remind us of the devotion Israelite wives demonstrated in encouraging their husbands to continue having children and not to lose hope in the future during the dark days of slavery, because the apple tree (whose fruit is the main ingredient of [*haroset*]) is mentioned in the context of marital intimacy in Song of Songs 8:5—understood homiletically as referring to the period of slavery in Egypt."

Fourth Question: "Why is it that on all other nights we either sit or recline at the table, but on this night we eat in a reclining position?"

Answer: Though Jews are familiar with this question because of its inclusion in the Four Questions, outside of the Orthodox world most Jews do not assume a reclining position at the Seder table (which usually involves the placing of a pillow on one's seat). The reason Jews are instructed to recline is that in the time of the Roman Empire, the dominant world power when the Haggadah was formally composed, free men reclined at the table. Therefore, eating in a reclining position came to symbolize luxury and freedom.

For Discussion
Four Adult Questions

Now that the children have asked their questions, adults might wish to ask and discuss questions of their own. Here are four with which one might start:

1. Given that our society is overwhelmingly secular, why should I take God and religion seriously?

2. If God took the Jews out of Egypt in Pharaoh's time, why didn't He take them out of Europe during Hitler's time?

3. Must the Seder be a religious experience, or is it enough for it to be a family and/or national Jewish experience?

4. Given that Jews make up two-tenths of 1 percent of the world's population—or, to put it another way, 99.8 percent of the world is not Jewish—why is it so important that the Jews and Judaism survive and that I help keep them alive?

The purpose of these questions is to stimulate discussion among the Seder participants. In light of that, the following answers are my answers, not "the right" answers. Nor are they the entirety of what I would answer. They are listed here to stimulate further discussion.

An answer to Question 1:

Only if there is a God is there ultimate meaning to life. If there is no God, everything that exists does so as a result of random chance, including, of course, every human being. See the discussion about the centrality of God under "God, Not Moses, Is Credited with the Exodus" (page 30).

An answer to Question 2:

One can ask the identical question regarding other nations' mass murders: the forty to sixty million Chinese killed by Mao's communist regime; the twenty to thirty million murdered by Stalin's communist regime, including six million Ukrainians; the one out of four Cambodians killed by Pol Pot and his communist regime; the mass killings of Armenians by the Ottoman Turks; the slaughter of Tutsis by Hutus in Rwanda; and so many others. And since every life is infinitely precious, one can also ask this question about any individual unjustly murdered: Why didn't God intervene to stop it?

The most honest answer is that God allows bad things to happen to good people because God has given human beings free will. If God were to intervene to save every individual who was about to be hurt by another human being, human beings as we know them would not exist. For one thing, humans would be robots. For another, if evil were not possible, nor would good be possible: if all we could do was good, acts of goodness would be no more "good" than breathing.

Returning to the specifically Jewish question posed here: Why didn't God intervene in the Holocaust (or, for that matter, during any of the innumerable atrocities committed against Jews throughout history) as He did during the Exodus?

In attempting an answer, it is important to bear in mind that God allowed centuries to elapse before intervening to end the Jews' suffering in Egypt. For hundreds of years, He allowed their enslavement, and He did nothing to prevent the murder of their baby boys when Pharaoh felt threatened enough by their numbers to order that all male Hebrew newborns be thrown into the Nile. So, then, if we are to attribute the end of the Egyptian enslavement to God's intervention, we could also attribute the end of the Holocaust to God's intervention. Of course, it doesn't explain why God first allowed six million Jews to be murdered—but neither does the Exodus explain why God first allowed generations of Jews to suffer and, near the end, the baby boys to be killed.

All we can say for certain is that the Jewish people survived Pharaoh and the Jewish people survived Hitler and the Nazis. Does God have a hand in the survival of the Jewish people? I believe so. Of course, it's a belief—it cannot be proven, but it is the best explanation for the Jews' utterly unlikely survival across three thousand years, something no other people dispersed from its homeland achieved.

Finally, nowhere in the Torah is it implied that God will prevent the murder of a single Jew. What the Torah does promise is that God will never allow the whole Jewish people to be annihilated.

> *The most important Jewish question, therefore, is not only whether the Seder needs to have a religious component but whether being a Jew needs to have a religious component.*

An answer to Question 3:

At the time of this writing, more Jews attend a Passover Seder than participate in any other Jewish activity, including attending synagogue on Rosh Hashanah or Yom Kippur. This is as true for secular Jews outside of Israel as it is for secular Israeli Jews. Since living in Israel serves to maintain the Jewish identity of many secular Israeli Jews, and since family life in Israel is quite strong, one can foresee non-religious Israelis attending Seders for the indefinite future. However, the same cannot be said about most irreligious Jews outside of Israel. It is difficult to imagine that secular Seders will last long outside of an Israeli context. This, then, is one reason to involve God and religious ritual in one's Seder: to maximize the chances that one's children and grandchildren continue having a Seder. The most important Jewish question, therefore, is not only whether the Seder needs to have a religious component but whether being a Jew needs to have a religious component.

An answer to Question 4:

For Discussion
Why Be a Jew?

This is the most important question in Jewish life. Why be Jewish? Why should someone born a Jew identify as a Jew and lead a Jewish life, and why should someone searching for a religion be Jewish?

In the modern world there are innumerable options: other religions, secular "-isms" that function as religions, and atheism. Yet modern Jewish life has rarely given Jews rational answers to this question. It has been preoccupied with answering the question of how to be a Jew, not why. But without a why, the how eventually becomes irrelevant.

Let us begin by excluding a reason that many Jews give when trying to inspire a young Jew to retain a Jewish identity: pride in Jewish achievement—which usually means pride in the achievements of modern Jews, not pride in the Jews' having given the world God, the Bible, ethical monotheism (a God whose primary demand is that humans behave ethically), and the Ten Commandments, among other world-shaping values.

A typical example is Jewish pride in the disproportionate number of Jews who have won a Nobel Prize. However, it is hard to imagine any young Jew deciding to lead a Jewish life because of the number of Jews awarded a Nobel Prize.

I first realized how unconvincing this line of argument was to me when I turned thirteen. One of the gifts I received for my bar-mitzvah was a book titled *Great Jews in Sports* (I remember it being somewhat thin, with large print and big pictures). Though I followed sports, I remember thinking: *What difference does it make?* Why should it matter to me that some great baseball players or boxers were Jews?

So I begin this list of reasons to be Jewish by excluding what many people might mention—pride in Jews' achievements. I have pride in the Jewish achievement of shaping the world through the Torah. That defines my Jewish pride. And, more important, it gives my life purpose and meaning: to continue to shape the world through the Torah.

In making the case for being or becoming a Jew, the first word that comes to mind is "Shabbat." If I had to make a sales pitch for Judaism, I would begin with Shabbat. If I were allowed only one reason for someone to lead a Jewish life, I would say "Shabbat." If I were to encourage a Jew to engage in one Jewish ritual, it would be Shabbat.

It is not possible to take Shabbat seriously and not become a changed person as well as a serious Jew. I will add that it is an immeasurable loss to America and to Christianity that the Sabbath is not taken seriously. When I was a young boy, it was taken quite seriously. No stores were open on Sunday—and this was in Brooklyn, New York, not Des Moines, Iowa. Life was palpably different on Sunday. There was little traffic—where were you going to go? And people dressed up. Everywhere there was a church, people dressed beautifully, in what was known as their "Sunday best." Then the 1960s came, the Sabbath began to die, and most people who did attend church stopped wearing their "Sunday best."

Shabbat is not only a life-prolonger, it is a life-fulfiller. The alternative—every day essentially the same, Friday night as a repeat of the other nights of the week and Saturday as a repeat of the other days of the week—is, to those of us who have Shabbat, thoroughly depressing.

To someone considering Judaism, this is my first argument: you will have Shabbat. And by the way, God seems to think so, too: It is the only ritual in the Ten Commandments. Kosher isn't in the Ten Commandments. Nor is Yom Kippur. Not one ritual except for Shabbat.

If the Jews did nothing else distinctly Jewish, the Jews would survive thanks to Shabbat alone. Nor is any other ritual as transformative as Shabbat. Kashrut doesn't transform your life nearly as much as Shabbat does. To leave the world of work and politics and video games for a day each week and spend it with family and/or friends is Judaism's greatest gift to the Jews and to the world. The power of Shabbat in keeping the family together also cannot be overstated. Every week of the year, families (and/or friends) sit down to share an elaborate meal which usually goes on for hours. Friday night and Saturday are sacred family time. Shabbat is by far my most positive family memory of my childhood. The Seder is a powerful and positive memory. But that was once a year. Shabbat is every week.

My second argument for being Jewish is the Torah. The best way I can articulate the power of the Torah is with this sentiment: I do not believe in the Torah because I believe in God, I believe in God because I believe in the Torah. Studying the Torah is my way of encountering God—even more so, for me personally, than prayer. I believe God's words are in the Torah. Indeed, I've worked much of my life making that case.

The Torah does something else for me.

I need to have my mind engaged, not just my emotions. That's one of the reasons I love classical music. Classical music touches my heart; I often have tears at the end of, let's say, a Brahms symphony. But classical music engages my mind, not just my emotions. That's part of the reason I love it. And the Torah does the same—it engages both my intellect and my emotions. The Torah is so intelligent and wise, my mind is fulfilled in studying it. For too many people in all religions, their religiosity is rooted in emotions, not the intellect.

Number three, by being a Jew you are sustaining or joining the Chosen People. Chosenness is not some abstract theological term for me. I believe that God chose this people to take His message to the world: belief in the Ten Commandments and in a universal God Who demands moral behavior and Who judges every individual accordingly.

Being a member of the Chosen People is open to anybody. Judaism has always, from the outset, welcomed the non-ethnic Hebrew into the Jewish people. The first Jew, Abraham, was a convert. The Messiah in Judaism will descend from a convert, Ruth. Many non-Jews left Egypt with the Jews. *Erev rav* is the Torah's term for the mixed multitudes who went out with the Hebrews from Egypt; they received the same Ten Commandments at Sinai and experienced the same visions of God. There has never been, ethnically speaking, a "pure" Jew. We don't all come from Abraham, but even if we did, Abraham himself wasn't a "pure" Jew.

If you take Chosenness seriously, it is life-transforming and, ultimately, world-transforming. One of the tragedies of modern Judaism is that rabbis rarely emphasize Jewish Chosenness. In any given year, how many rabbis speak about the Jews being Chosen and what that means?

Number four: I am passionate about Judaism generally and the Torah specifically for their emphasis on goodness and morality. After graduating from a yeshiva high school, I continued studying Judaism at the yeshiva's metivta (post-graduate academy) under the school's remarkable principal, Rabbi David Eliach. I once asked him his take on ethical monotheism. His response permanently influenced me. "Judaism," he said, "*is* ethical monotheism, and ethical monotheism *is* Judaism."

God wants us to be good. That is the message of Judaism. It is staggeringly simple. The proof is that, according to Judaism, every good person shares in the world to come. That should be a very big selling point for Judaism. There's no clearer illustration of a religion's emphasis on goodness and morality than its asserting that God doesn't judge a non-Jew's theology, only his behavior.

Those are pretty big selling points: Shabbat, Torah, the mission of the Chosen People, the emphasis on being good, and the appeal to the mind as well as the heart.

And all those lead to the fifth reason: Judaism fills one's life with meaning.

Meaning, as Viktor Frankl, the great Jewish psychoanalyst who survived Auschwitz, said, is the greatest human need, even more so than the erotic drive. There are many people who lead celibate but nevertheless happy lives, but no one is happy whose life lacks meaning.

Having God and religion in one's life, having a mission, having a community (one of Judaism's other strong points)—these fill a committed Jew's life with meaning.

In a nutshell, just as God keeps the Jewish people alive in the world, the Jewish people keep God alive in the world. This is true even though most modern Jews are secular. The continuity of the Jews and their return to Israel after 1,900 years in exile bear testimony both to the existence of God and to the validity of His promises.

The answers offered here do not mean that there are no secular answers to the question of why it should matter if the Jews survive as a distinct people. But it is harder to provide persuasive secular answers than persuasive religious ones to this question. Therefore, non-religious Jews at the Seder ought to try to answer this question, and this may help: How much do the secular Jews at the Seder care if their children and grandchildren identify as Jews? And if they do care, why?

Answering the Four Questions:
The Narrative of the Haggadah

עֲבָדִים הָיִינוּ לְפַרְעֹה בְּמִצְרָיִם,

We were slaves to Pharaoh in the land of Egypt.

The paragraph opens with the words: "We were slaves to Pharaoh in the land of Egypt." Note that it says "*We* were slaves," not "*They* were slaves." Nothing illustrates the secret of Jewish continuity better than the pronoun "we." To provide an American example, on July 4, the American Independence Day, Americans would do well to say, "We rebelled against Great Britain."

As long as Jews speak in terms of "we," the Passover story will remain every Jew's story.

For Discussion
Was There Really an Exodus?

There are Jews who argue that the Exodus never took place, that the story of the Jews enslaved in Egypt is a fable. Some of these are committed Jews who celebrate the Seder. They maintain that what matters is not whether the Exodus happened but what the story teaches.

However, both theologically and historically, Judaism and Jewish survival rest as much on the Exodus as on the Creation. Arguing that it is not necessary for Jews to believe their ancestors were enslaved in Egypt is Jewishly no different than arguing it is not necessary for Jews to believe that God created the world. Moreover, given the centrality of the Exodus to the Torah, to say it didn't happen would make the entirety of the Torah suspect.

Judaism and Jewish survival ultimately depend upon those two faith statements. That is why the Jewish liturgy speaks of *zikaron lima'a'seh bereshit* ("commemorating the works of Creation") and *zecher litziat mitzrayim* ("commemorating the Exodus from Egypt").

Belief in the Exodus is not a function of blind faith. Both history and common sense argue for its historicity. A major (non-Orthodox) biblical scholar, Richard Elliott

Friedman, professor of Jewish Studies at the University of Georgia, framed the issue of the historicity of the Exodus beautifully: "*Something happened.* It may not have included the sun going dark for three days or sticks turning to snakes. It may not have had two million people. But it did include some core of the future people of Israel departing Egypt."

Here are some of Friedman's arguments:

- Do you really think that the Israelites made up a story that they were descended from slaves?
- Do you think that they completely made up a story that they were not indigenous in their land—that they had become a people someplace else?
- Do you think that they made up Moses?
- Do you think that they made up a story that Moses had a Midianite priest as his father-in-law?
- Are four hundred years of presence of Western Semites as aliens in Egypt, and then those fifty-two references about how to treat aliens, a coincidence?
- Do you think that not finding 3,300-year-old evidence in the Sinai wilderness in surveys in the twenty-first century outweighs all of this?
- Were fifty-two references to being good to aliens and four times saying that this was "because we were aliens in Egypt" unrelated to ever having actually been in Egypt?

If the Jews were never in Egypt, the phrase "because you were strangers in Egypt" would have struck them as absurd and incomprehensible.

This last argument is particularly compelling. The Torah repeatedly commands the Jews to love the stranger, and each time it adds the words, "because you were strangers in Egypt." If the Jews were never in Egypt, the phrase "because you were strangers in Egypt" would have struck them as absurd and incomprehensible.

I would offer one additional argument on behalf of the historicity of the Jews being enslaved in Egypt and finally escaping it. The Torah includes too many details of ancient Egyptian life to assume people writing centuries later—people who had no contact with Egypt—would have been acquainted with these details.

For Discussion
Does Judaism Rest on Any Doctrines of Faith?

Judaism rests on two pillars of faith, Creation and Exodus: God as the Creator of the universe and God as the Liberator of the Jews from Egypt. Had the Jews abandoned either belief, they would not have remained Jews. They would have disappeared, as has every other nation that was exiled from its homeland. Shabbat commemorates the Creation. In the Book of Exodus, the Fourth Commandment gives Creation as the reason for Shabbat: "For in six days He created the Heavens and the Earth and on the Seventh Day He rested." Therefore, we are to rest on the Seventh Day each week to remind ourselves and the world that God created the world.

In the same way Shabbat commemorates the Creation, Passover commemorates the Exodus. Moreover, in Moses's recounting of the Ten Commandments in Deuteronomy (5:12–15), the last Book of the Torah, Shabbat commemorates not the Creation but the Exodus. That is how important the Exodus is to Judaism. Both Shabbat and Passover commemorate the Exodus.

For Discussion
Is It Possible to Instill Empathy in People?

Another reason for saying "we" is to instill a greater degree of empathy in the speaker. Clearly, one is more likely to empathize with people described as "we" than people described as "they." The further removed one is from identifying with others' suffering, the less one feels it. Presumably, a Chinese parent who tells his or her child about the deaths of between forty and sixty million Chinese in the communist-induced famine of the 1950s will say "we," whereas a non-Chinese will say "they."

Nevertheless, we need to acknowledge that while sympathy is possible and desirable, complete empathy is impossible. Unless one has endured the same experience—whether in terms of pleasure or pain—one can *imagine* what it would be like, but not truly empathize.

Every one of us can *imagine* the pain of a parent who has lost a child, but only those who have lost a child can empathize with a person who has. I learned this from a man whose twenty-one-year-old son was killed in a car crash. Many years later, I asked him if anything had ever helped him heal.

He responded that nothing—not psychotherapy, not religion, not even close friends—had helped reduce his grief. The one thing that finally helped him was regularly meeting with other parents who had lost a child—because, he explained, only people who had lost a child could empathize with him.

I myself learned this truth about empathy after a period of serious, sometimes disabling, physical pain. I realized that when listening to, or reading about, other people's pain, one can, and of course should, *sympathize* with them, but unless one has experienced similar pain, it is not possible to truly *empathize* with them. It is like telling people in sub-Saharan Africa about the pain of freezing in the Russian winter, or telling men about the pain of childbirth.

Instilling Empathy in Children

While it is impossible to have complete empathy with others, it is critical to attempt to instill as much empathy as possible in one's children. Individuals with empathy are far less likely to inflict gratuitous suffering on others, and a lack of empathy is a defining characteristic of the sociopath. That is one reason parents should punish their children when they hurt others. By experiencing the pain of punishment, children will hopefully begin to understand the pain they have inflicted.

Empathy also helps explain why it is neither wrong nor evidence of a mean character to want those who deliberately inflict unjust suffering to experience similar suffering. Most people intuitively understand that unless evildoers experience some of the pain they have inflicted on others—that is, empathize in some way with their victims—they will never begin to understand the horror of what they have done.

Empathy is so important that it is one of the solutions to the problem of human evil. If people identified with others, they would be far less likely to inflict unjust suffering on them. (I write "unjust suffering" because there is such a thing as "just suffering." Punishment of criminals is one such example.)

Suffering Doesn't Always Engender Empathy

All this notwithstanding, even though suffering theoretically confers the ability to empathize with similar suffering on the part of others, it does not guarantee empathy. Many people who suffer do not develop either empathy or the decent behavior empathy should engender. For example, people who have suffered at the hands of others have two options: they can use their anger over their suffering to legitimize making others suffer, or they can use the memory of their suffering to prevent others from experiencing such pain. *Suffering ennobles only those who want to be ennobled by it.*

God, Not Moses, Is Credited with the Exodus

וַיּוֹצִיאֵנוּ ה' אֱלֹהֵינוּ מִשָּׁם בְּיָד חֲזָקָה וּבִזְרֹעַ נְטוּיָה. וְאִלּוּ לֹא הוֹצִיא הַקָּדוֹשׁ
בָּרוּךְ הוּא אֶת אֲבוֹתֵינוּ מִמִּצְרַיִם, הֲרֵי אָנוּ וּבָנֵינוּ וּבְנֵי בָנֵינוּ מְשֻׁעְבָּדִים הָיִינוּ
לְפַרְעֹה בְּמִצְרָיִם.

And the Lord, our God, took us out from there with a strong hand and an outstretched forearm. And if the Holy One, blessed be He, had not taken our ancestors from Egypt, behold we and our children and our children's children would [all] be enslaved to Pharaoh in Egypt.

For Discussion
Why Isn't Moses Mentioned in the Haggadah?

Answer: because it was God who took the Jews out of Egypt.

Incredibly, despite Moses's enormous role in the Exodus, he is not yet mentioned in the Haggadah. In fact, except for one mention in a psalm recited later in the Seder, *Moses is never mentioned in the Haggadah*. Moses, the man God chose to lead the Jews out of Egypt, the most important Jewish leader in Jewish history and one of the most influential individuals in world history, is not mentioned in the liturgy of the holiday commemorating the Exodus.

Though incredible, the reason is not hard to fathom. The Rabbis wanted Jews never to forget that it was God Who brought them out from Egypt. To put it another way, had there been no Moses, God would still have taken the Jews out of Egypt. And if it weren't for God, the Jews would not have been taken out of Egypt.

From the beginning, Jewish Scripture sought to prevent worship of Moses. That is almost surely why God did not allow Moses to enter the Promised Land. Most people with any acquaintance with the Bible believe God denied Moses entry into Israel because Moses hit, rather than talked to, a rock from which water would miraculously flow and quench the thirst of the Jews in the desert.

But that understanding is incorrect. The reason God forbade Moses entry into the Promised Land was that Moses said to the Jews that "we" (he and his brother Aaron) would get the rock to produce water (see Numbers 20:2–13). By attributing the miracle to himself rather than to God, Moses might have led the Jews to attribute the Exodus to Moses rather than to God and ultimately to come to worship Moses.

For this reason, Moses died alone in view of, but outside, the Promised Land. Also for that reason, "no one knows his burial place" (Deuteronomy 34:6)—lest his burial place ever turn into a shrine. In addition, the Torah goes out of its way to depict Moses as a human being—a great human being, to be sure, but a human being with human flaws.

Walter Kaufmann, a professor of religion at Princeton, conjectured:

> Moses went away to die alone, lest any man should know his grave to worship there or attach any value to his mortal body. Having seen Egypt, he knew . . . how prone men are to such superstitions. [Ever since,] what the Jews have presented to the world has not been Moses or any individual, but their ideas about God and man. It is a measure of Moses's greatness that one cannot but imagine he would have approved wholeheartedly. It would have broken his heart if he had thought that his followers would build temples to make images of him or elevate him into heaven. That he has never been deified—like the Pharaoh of ancient Egypt—is one of the most significant facts about the ideas of God and man in the Old Testament.[3]

For Discussion
How Important Is God to Judaism?

God is the essence of Judaism. That many modern Jews are not particularly God-centered and many are agnostic or atheist only bears testimony to the fact that Jews and Judaism are not the same things. For example, most Jews do not observe the Sabbath, yet the Sabbath is so important, it is one of the Ten Commandments.

The purpose of Judaism is to live a moral life and a God-centered life (within Judaism the latter presumes the former), and the purpose of the Jews is to spread knowledge of the God of the Torah, the God of the Ten Commandments, and this God's moral demands throughout the world.

For Discussion
How Important Is God to Morality?

One reason God is so important to Judaism is that morality is so important to Judaism. Without God as the source of an objective morality and as the moral judge of every human, the world would devolve into moral chaos.

Without God there is no moral truth; there are only moral opinions.

Take murder, for example.

Is murder wrong? Is it evil? We can assume that every person at this Seder table would answer yes. But how do any of you *know* it is wrong? If you were asked, for example, "How do you know the earth is round?" you would show photographs from outer space and provide measurable data. But what photographs or measurements could you provide to prove that murder or rape or theft is wrong?

The fact is that no one can. Whether or not there is a God, there are scientific facts—because scientific facts are empirically provable. But moral facts are not empirically provable. If there is no God, there are no moral facts. Only if there is a God who says murder is wrong is it a fact that murder is wrong. (That God's existence is a matter of faith rather than fact in no way contradicts this last statement. That is why the sentence reads, "only *if* there is a God").

"But," you might say, "murder is wrong because I know that I wouldn't want to be murdered." This "Golden Rule"–based argument is widely cited, but it in no way makes murder objectively wrong. The fact that you wouldn't want something done to you doesn't mean that it is wrong. It means nothing more than you wouldn't want that thing done to you. But few murderers want to be murdered, no rapist wants to be raped, and no torturer wants to be tortured. But that fact hasn't stopped people from committing those acts. There has been a staggering amount of murder, rape, and torture in history. Hitler, Stalin, and Mao didn't want to be murdered, but that did not prevent them from murdering about a hundred million people.

Some might respond that people who believe in God have also committed such evils. That is certainly true, but no one is arguing that belief in God guarantees people will not commit evil. The argument is that without God, good and evil do not objectively exist.

Moreover, it was secular ideologies and secular regimes that made the twentieth century the bloodiest century in recorded history. Yes, religion has a lot to answer for, but the commonplace argument that "more people have been killed in the name of religion than in the name of anything else" was true only prior to the twentieth century—when just about everyone was religious. So, the claim doesn't prove much. Especially when one considers this:

Nearly all the moral good of the modern age was achieved in the West, the civilization rooted in the Bible, in Judeo-Christian values. The anti-slavery movement was founded and led by religious Christians in Britain and British colonists (and, after the American Revolution, American citizens) in North America—in the name of God. The civil rights movement in America was led by a religious Christian minister, the Reverend Martin Luther King Jr. The country most supportive of Israel has been the United States—thanks largely to how religious a country America has been. The proof is that as America becomes less religious, its support for Israel lessens. America, the freest country in world history, was founded by Bible-centered and God-centered men who all believed that *God wants humans to be free*. This is not a defense of all Christians in the West, many of whom in North and South America defended slavery and many of whom in Europe failed when confronted with Nazi antisemitism. But the unique moral achievements of the modern world—free speech, free elections, women's equality, the end of slavery, to cite a few—were products of the Judeo-Christian West.

Without God, the words "good" and "evil" are just another way of saying "I like" and "I don't like."

One thing is certain: when Christianity died in Europe, fascism, Nazism, and communism took its place. If Christianity dies in America, what will replace it?

Two additional things need to be made clear.

First, none of this means that if you don't believe in God, you can't be a good person. There are kind and moral individuals who do not believe in God. But the existence of these good people is irrelevant to the question of whether good and evil objectively exist if there is no God. There have always been good individuals, in every culture. There were undoubtedly good individuals who believed in Zeus. But they were good despite their belief in Zeus, not because of it. And most important, a good and decent society cannot be made if the society believes in Zeus rather than in the God of the Bible.

Second, none of this means that everyone who believes in God is a good person; indeed, more than a few have been evil—and have even committed evil in God's name. The existence of God doesn't ensure people will do good. I wish it did. The existence of God only ensures that good and evil objectively exist and are not merely opinions.

Without God, we therefore end up with what is known as moral relativism—meaning that morality is not absolute, but only relative to the individual or to the society. Without

God, the words "good" and "evil" are just another way of saying "I like" and "I don't like." If there is no God, the statement "Murder is evil" is the same as the statement "I don't like murder."

In the *New York Times*, a professor of philosophy confirmed this: "The overwhelming majority of college freshmen . . . view moral claims as mere opinions."

In fact, it is worse than that:

> What would you say if you found out that our public schools were teaching children that it is not true that it's wrong to kill people for fun. . . ? Would you be surprised?
>
> I was. As a philosopher, I already knew that many college-aged students don't believe in moral facts. While there are no national surveys quantifying this phenomenon, philosophy professors with whom I have spoken suggest that the overwhelming majority of college freshmen in their classrooms view moral claims as mere opinions that are not true or are true only relative to a culture.[4]

In order to make moral individuals and a moral society, Judaism goes far beyond claiming that good and evil objectively exist. Judaism posits a God who commands us to be good and lays out what good is: first with the Ten Commandments, and then in an elaborate system of laws such as "Love your neighbor as yourself," "Love the stranger," and even "Do not muzzle an ox while it works in the field."

For Discussion
How Important Is God to Meaning in Life?

If there is no God, life has no ultimate meaning. The godless universe is bereft of meaning, oblivious to our existence, and pitiless. "Without God, life has no meaning & death is the end. . . . [The universe] has no design, no purpose, no evil, no good, nothing but pitiless indifference." Those are the words of one of the most famous atheists of the contemporary world, physicist Richard Dawkins. And the human being, he has written, is nothing more than a "throwaway survival machine."

The most prominent atheist philosopher of the twentieth century, Bertrand Russell, likewise wrote: "I have not written in anything about 'The meaning or purpose of life.' Unless you assume a God, the question is meaningless. . . ."[5]

The crisis of the modern world—an increasingly godless, secular world—is the loss of meaning. But human beings cannot live without meaning, and therein lies the greatest modern problem: how to find meaning in a world deemed meaningless. The secular doctrines, such as Nazism and the offshoots of Marxism, that have filled that void have led to moral chaos. Judaism provided the Jew—and the world—with the answer: following God's moral commandments (and for the Jew, the ritual commandments as well) and spreading God-based ethics—ethical monotheism—to the rest of the world.

For Discussion
How Important Is God to Human Worth?

If there is no God, human beings are just as Dawkins described them—"throwaway survival machines." Judaism gave the world the concept that humans are precious when it described man as "created in the image of God" (Genesis 1:27). Without God, the unique preciousness of human beings is also lost.

Even Scholars and the Most Wise Must Retell the Story of the Exodus on This Night

וַאֲפִילוּ כֻּלָּנוּ חֲכָמִים כֻּלָּנוּ נְבוֹנִים כֻּלָּנוּ זְקֵנִים כֻּלָּנוּ יוֹדְעִים אֶת הַתּוֹרָה מִצְוָה עָלֵינוּ לְסַפֵּר בִּיצִיאַת מִצְרָיִם. וְכָל הַמַּרְבֶּה לְסַפֵּר בִּיצִיאַת מִצְרַיִם הֲרֵי זֶה מְשֻׁבָּח.

The late Rabbi Jonathan Sacks noted that the French and Russian Revolutions, initiated by godless intellectuals, were violent and murderous in the extreme, in contrast with the far more peaceful American Revolution initiated by God-affirming intellectuals.

And even if we were all sages, all discerning, all elders, all knowledgeable about the Torah, it would be a commandment upon us to tell the story of the Exodus from Egypt. And anyone who adds [and spends extra time] in telling the story of the Exodus from Egypt, behold he is praiseworthy.

To illustrate the point, the Haggadah then relates a story about five great rabbis:

מַעֲשֶׂה בְּרַבִּי אֱלִיעֶזֶר וְרַבִּי יְהוֹשֻׁעַ וְרַבִּי אֶלְעָזָר בֶּן־עֲזַרְיָה וְרַבִּי עֲקִיבָא וְרַבִּי טַרְפוֹן שֶׁהָיוּ מְסֻבִּין בִּבְנֵי־בְרַק וְהָיוּ מְסַפְּרִים בִּיצִיאַת מִצְרַיִם כָּל־אוֹתוֹ הַלַּיְלָה, עַד שֶׁבָּאוּ תַלְמִידֵיהֶם וְאָמְרוּ לָהֶם רַבּוֹתֵינוּ הִגִּיעַ זְמַן קְרִיאַת שְׁמַע שֶׁל שַׁחֲרִית.

It happened once [on Pesach] that Rabbi Eliezer, Rabbi Yehoshua, Rabbi Elazar ben Azariah, Rabbi Akiva, and Rabbi Tarfon were reclining in Bnei Brak and were telling the story of the Exodus from Egypt that whole night, until their students came and said to them, "The time of [reciting] the morning Shema has arrived."

All of these five rabbis were, in Rabbi Shmuel Goldin's words, "towering scholars of great renown, clearly familiar with the Exodus narrative in all its details." This, then, is another extraordinarily important lesson imparted by the Haggadah. No brilliant intellectual should ever consider himself too good or too bright to avoid doing what the rest of the people have to do. The alienation of intellectuals from the common men and women among their people has caused great harm in the modern world. Virtually every bad modern idea originated among secular intellectuals. The late Rabbi Jonathan Sacks noted that the French and Russian Revolutions, initiated by godless intellectuals, were violent and murderous in the extreme, in contrast with the far more peaceful American Revolution initiated by God-affirming intellectuals.

אָמַר רַבִּי אֶלְעָזָר בֶּן־עֲזַרְיָה הֲרֵי אֲנִי כְּבֶן שִׁבְעִים שָׁנָה וְלֹא זָכִיתִי שֶׁתֵּאָמֵר יְצִיאַת מִצְרַיִם בַּלֵּילוֹת עַד שֶׁדְּרָשָׁהּ בֶּן זוֹמָא, שֶׁנֶּאֱמַר, לְמַעַן תִּזְכֹּר אֶת יוֹם צֵאתְךָ מֵאֶרֶץ מִצְרַיִם כֹּל יְמֵי חַיֶּיךָ. יְמֵי חַיֶּיךָ הַיָּמִים. כֹּל יְמֵי חַיֶּיךָ הַלֵּילוֹת.

Rabbi Elazar ben Azariah said, "Behold I am like a man of seventy years and I have not merited [to understand why] the Exodus from Egypt should be said at night until Ben Zoma explicated it, as it is stated (Deuteronomy 16:3), 'In order that you remember the day of your going out from the land of Egypt all the days of your life'; 'the days of your life' [indicates that the remembrance be invoked during] the days, 'all the days of your life' [indicates that the remembrance be invoked also during] the nights."

וַחֲכָמִים אוֹמְרִים יְמֵי חַיֶּיךָ הָעוֹלָם הַזֶּה. כֹּל יְמֵי חַיֶּיךָ לְהָבִיא לִימוֹת הַמָּשִׁיחַ.

But the Sages say, 'The days of your life' [refer to] this world; 'all the days of your life' [refer to] the days of the Messiah.

For Discussion
Does Judaism Affirm the Afterlife? Does Reason?

The last statement of this prayer speaks of this life and an afterlife. This is an affirmation of the Jewish belief in an afterlife.

Many Jews do not believe in an afterlife and believe that Judaism doesn't either. I once attended a funeral at which a prominent rabbi officiated. To probably everyone present, nothing unusual occurred; the service was a traditional one and the remarks made by the rabbi about the deceased were moving.

Then, at the grave, the rabbi spoke about Judaism's attitude toward death. "Judaism does not believe in a life after death," he said. "Rather, we live on in the good works we do and in the memories of those we leave behind."

Because this is what many contemporary Jews believe, few people at the funeral found reason to take particular notice of these remarks. But what the rabbi said was incorrect.

Jews who believe that there is no reality beyond death are certainly entitled to hold such a belief. They may even be right. But that is their belief, not what Judaism teaches. The entry under "Afterlife" in the scholarly and secular *Encyclopedia Judaica* begins, "Judaism has always maintained a belief in an afterlife." See, among many examples, the eleventh chapter of the Talmudic tractate *Sanhedrin* and Maimonides's *Thirteen Principles of Faith*.

It is true that the Torah and even later Judaism give no details about what happens after death. Judaism wants its adherents to focus on this world. One reason Judaism prohibits its priests from coming into contact with the dead—a prohibition that may be unique among the world's religions—is that a Jewish priest's focus must be on this world and life, not on the next world and death.

But the affirmation of this world does not mean this life is all there is.

Since Judaism and all monotheistic religions are predicated upon the existence of a God Who is nonphysical and beyond nature, and Who is just and loving, our physical existence cannot be the only reality. It is implausible that a just and loving God would create a world wherein the sum total of His creations' existence is unjust suffering. To state this case as starkly as possible, if there is nothing after this life, the Nazis and their victims have identical fates. If I believed such a thing, I would either become an atheist or hate the god who had created such a cruel and absurd universe.

As for the rabbi's statement that we live on through the memories of loved ones, what would the rabbi say about the millions of Jews whose loved ones also died during the Holocaust? If people live on solely through the memories of their loved ones, then, obviously, many of the six million did not live on. They are nothing more than forgotten smoke. Meanwhile, the evil that people do often does live on.

Those who wish to believe that this life is all there is should acknowledge that this belief renders the lives of many people little more than a cruel joke.

Furthermore, those who believe that this life is the only reality are likely to be led to one or more of three negative conclusions about life:

1. Hedonism: If this life is all one has, it is quite logical to live a life devoted to self-gratification. If the physical is the only reality, we should experience as much physical

pleasure as possible. To paraphrase an old beer slogan, the message is, "You only go around once in life, so get all the gusto you can."

2. Utopianism: Not all people who believe this life is all there is affirm hedonism. But many of these embrace a considerably more dangerous ideology: utopianism, the desire to make heaven on earth (given that there is no other heaven). Hence the attraction of utopianism to so many twentieth-century radicals who rejected Judaism and Christianity. In light of the hells on earth that secular utopians have produced, it should be clear just how important it is to defer Utopia to a God-made future world.

3. Despair: Considering the great physical and emotional pain that so many people experience, what is more likely to induce despondency than the belief that this life is all there is? The malaise felt by so many people living in modern society is not traceable to material deprivation but, in large part, to the despair induced by the belief that this world is all there is. That is why peasants with religious faith are often happier than affluent people who have no faith.

The Four Sons

בָּרוּךְ הַמָּקוֹם, בָּרוּךְ הוּא, בָּרוּךְ שֶׁנָּתַן תּוֹרָה לְעַמּוֹ יִשְׂרָאֵל, בָּרוּךְ הוּא. כְּנֶגֶד
אַרְבָּעָה בָנִים דִּבְּרָה תוֹרָה: אֶחָד חָכָם, וְאֶחָד רָשָׁע, וְאֶחָד תָּם, וְאֶחָד שֶׁאֵינוֹ
יוֹדֵעַ לִשְׁאוֹל.

Blessed be The Place [God], blessed be He; blessed be the One Who Gave the Torah to His people Israel, blessed be He. Corresponding to four sons did the Torah speak: one who is wise, one who is wicked, one who is innocent, and one who doesn't know to ask.

As there are many types of children, our approaches to them must be tailored accordingly. To their credit, the ancient rabbis understood that children—even in the same family—are all different.

The four children identified in the Haggadah are the wise child, the wicked child, the simple child, and the child who doesn't know how to ask. The Torah and the Haggadah offer different suggestions on how to address each child.

There are additional ways of understanding the Four Sons. One is that they represent generations of Jews in the modern era: the first generation is a wise generation; the second generation rebels and rejects Judaism; the third generation is a simple generation; the fourth generation does not even know how or what to ask. Yet another understanding is that of Benjamin Telushkin (the son of Rabbi Joseph Telushkin): these four children represent all of us at different stages of our lives.

For Discussion
The Problem of Goodness without Wisdom

Even as a child I could not understand why, if there is a bad son, there is no good son. It struck me as a glaring omission.

I came to understand the reason only when I was well into adulthood: the wise child is the good child—because goodness demands wisdom. The Haggadah is imparting one of the most important lessons of life. One can have all the good intentions in the world and be an extraordinarily kind person, but lacking wisdom, the well-known aphorism applies: the road to hell is paved with good intentions.

That is why a society that does not teach wisdom to its young will ultimately fail. A society that does not teach young people, to cite but three examples, that the greatest battle in their lives is with their own nature; that the heart is a terrible moral guide; and that, with few exceptions, they need to honor their parents even if they don't love them—that society will likely not long survive. Yet, for the most part, not teaching young people wisdom has been the case for several generations now. One reason is that we have valued knowledge as if it is the same as wisdom, even though they are almost entirely unrelated. As the saying goes: "Knowledge is knowing that a tomato is a fruit; wisdom is knowing not to put it in a fruit salad."

Another is that we have valued intelligence as if it, too, is commensurate with wisdom. And most important, too many parents think love is enough to raise good children. It is not. Parents need to raise children with wisdom as much as they do with love. Love without wisdom produces spoiled children.

For Discussion
Teach Children the History and Importance of Freedom

In four different verses, the Torah instructs parents to tell their children about the Exodus and how God made it possible. That this command is stated four times clearly implies that the Torah considers it of the utmost importance to teach one's children about the Exodus—and therefore about the importance of freedom.

Jonathan Sacks wrote:

> To defend a country you need an army, but to defend a civilization you need education. That is why Moses, [who] according to Rousseau [was] the world's greatest architect of a free society, spoke about the duty of parents in every generation to educate their children about why freedom matters and how it was achieved. . . .
>
> Freedom begins with what we teach our children. That is why Jews became a people whose passion is education, whose heroes are teachers and whose citadels are schools. Nowhere is this more evident than on Passover, when the entire ritual of handing on our story to the next generation is set in motion by the questions asked by a child. In every generation we need to cultivate afresh the habits of the heart that Tocqueville called "the apprenticeship of liberty."

The message of Passover remains as powerful as ever. Freedom is won not on the battlefield but in the classroom and the home. *Teach your children the history of freedom if you want them never to lose it* (italics added).[6]

At the time of this writing, this message is particularly relevant to Americans. In the post–World War II era, many American parents and teachers have failed to teach their children and students the history of the struggle for freedom and its unique importance.

The Wise Son

חָכָם מָה הוּא אוֹמֵר? מָה הָעֵדוֹת וְהַחֻקִּים וְהַמִּשְׁפָּטִים אֲשֶׁר צִוָּה ה' אֱלֹהֵינוּ אֶתְכֶם. וְאַף אַתָּה אֱמוֹר לוֹ כְּהִלְכוֹת הַפֶּסַח: אֵין מַפְטִירִין אַחַר הַפֶּסַח אֲפִיקוֹמָן.

> *The message of Passover remains as powerful as ever. Freedom is won not on the battlefield but in the classroom and the home. Teach your children the history of freedom if you want them never to lose it.*
> —Jonathan Sacks

What does the wise [son] say? "What are these testimonies, statutes and judgments that the Lord our God commanded you?" And you will say to him, as per the laws of the Pesach sacrifice, "We may not eat an afikoman [a dessert or other foods eaten after the meal] after [we are finished eating] the Pesach sacrifice."[7]

This is one of the four Torah verses that commands us to educate our children about the Exodus. This one, Deuteronomy 6:20, depicts the wise son: he is genuinely curious to learn about Passover and its laws.

The Wicked Son

רָשָׁע מָה הוּא אוֹמֵר? מָה הָעֲבוֹדָה הַזֹּאת לָכֶם? לָכֶם – וְלֹא לוֹ. וּלְפִי שֶׁהוֹצִיא אֶת עַצְמוֹ מִן הַכְּלָל כָּפַר בְּעִקָּר. וְאַף אַתָּה הַקְהֵה אֶת שִׁנָּיו וֶאֱמוֹר לוֹ: "בַּעֲבוּר זֶה עָשָׂה ה' לִי בְּצֵאתִי מִמִּצְרָיִם". לִי וְלֹא־לוֹ. אִלּוּ הָיָה שָׁם, לֹא הָיָה נִגְאָל.

What does the wicked one say? "What is this worship to you?" (Exodus 12:26). "To you" and not "to him." Since he excluded himself from the collective, he denied a central principle [of the Jewish faith—Jewish peoplehood]. Accordingly, you will blunt his teeth and say to him, "For the sake of this, did the Lord do [this] for me in my going out of Egypt."[8] *"For me" and not "for him." If he had been there, he would not have been saved.*

A more contemporary and accurate (though not literal) translation of the wicked son's question would be: "What is all of this worship stuff about?" The tone in Hebrew is contemptuous. This son is above it all.

The Simple Son

תָּם מָה הוּא אוֹמֵר? "מַה זֹּאת"? וְאָמַרְתָּ אֵלָיו "בְּחוֹזֶק יָד הוֹצִיאָנוּ ה' מִמִּצְרַיִם מִבֵּית עֲבָדִים".

What does the simple one say? "What is this?" And you will say to him, "With the strength of [His] hand did the Lord take us out from Egypt, from the house of slaves" (Exodus 13:14).

This response argues for Benjamin Telushkin's insight—that we are all one or more of the four sons at given times in our life. Personally, at this time in my life, I find the response to the simple son the best of all. It is quite enough for me to believe that God took the Jews out of Egypt to sustain my religious faith. The moment you believe that, your life changes: you believe that there is a God, that God cares about His creations, and that God acts in history.

The Son Who Doesn't Know How to Ask

וְשֶׁאֵינוֹ יוֹדֵעַ לִשְׁאוֹל – אַתְּ פְּתַח לוֹ, שֶׁנֶּאֱמַר, וְהִגַּדְתָּ לְבִנְךָ בַּיּוֹם הַהוּא לֵאמֹר, בַּעֲבוּר זֶה עָשָׂה ה' לִי בְּצֵאתִי מִמִּצְרָיִם.

And [regarding] the one who doesn't know to ask, you will open [the conversation] for him. As it is stated (Exodus 13:8): "And you will speak to your son on that day saying, for the sake of this, did the Lord do [this] for me in my going out of Egypt."

יָכוֹל מֵרֹאשׁ חֹדֶשׁ? תַּלְמוּד לוֹמַר בַּיּוֹם הַהוּא. אִי בַּיּוֹם הַהוּא יָכוֹל מִבְּעוֹד יוֹם? תַּלְמוּד לוֹמַר בַּעֲבוּר זֶה – בַּעֲבוּר זֶה לֹא אָמַרְתִּי, אֶלָּא בְּשָׁעָה שֶׁיֵּשׁ מַצָּה וּמָרוֹר מֻנָּחִים לְפָנֶיךָ.

It could be from Rosh Chodesh [the New Month, that one would have to discuss the Exodus. However] we learn [otherwise, since] it is stated, "on that day." If it is [written] "on that day," it could be from while it is still day [before the night of the fifteenth of Nissan. However] we learn [otherwise, since] it is stated, "for the sake of this." I didn't say "for the sake of this" except [that it be observed] when [this] matzah *and* maror *are resting in front of you [meaning, on the night of the fifteenth].*

This paragraph relates a rabbinical question concerning precisely when the telling of the Exodus story should begin—in the evening or during the day? On the fourteenth of the Hebrew month of Nisan, when the Pesach (paschal) sacrifice took place (in the daytime), or on the fifteenth (in the evening), when the Exodus began? They resolve that it should be told in the evening, "when this *matzah* and *maror* are resting in front of you."

The Jews Began as Primitive
as All Other Peoples

מִתְּחִלָּה עוֹבְדֵי עֲבוֹדָה זָרָה הָיוּ אֲבוֹתֵינוּ,

Originally, our ancestors were idol worshipers.

The narrative part of the Seder does not begin with the Exodus, but with the Jews' origins. There is no attempt in the Torah, the rest of the Bible, or later Judaism to romanticize the Jews or their history. The Torah repeatedly emphasizes that the Jews were no better than any other people. This statement—that our ancestors were idol worshippers—is one such example.

Two reasons for this description of the Jews are:

1. The Torah is committed to truth. Thus, the Jews are regularly depicted as flawed. This is one of the reasons I believe the Torah and the Hebrew Bible. No holy work of any religion depicts its adherents as negatively as the Bible depicts the Jews. This is also a major reason I believe God is the ultimate Author of the Torah. If men (and/or women) had written the Torah, it is extremely unlikely the Jews would have been depicted as negatively as they are.

2. By emphasizing the Jews' unimpressive origins, the Torah makes clear that whatever eventual success and influence the Jewish people achieve cannot be attributed to any inherent superiority. The Jews went from a small, insignificant, and pagan people to shape the world solely because of God and Torah.

וְעַכְשָׁיו קֵרְבָנוּ הַמָּקוֹם לַעֲבֹדָתוֹ, שֶׁנֶּאֱמַר: וַיֹּאמֶר יְהוֹשֻׁעַ אֶל־כָּל־הָעָם, כֹּה אָמַר ה' אֱלֹהֵי יִשְׂרָאֵל: בְּעֵבֶר הַנָּהָר יָשְׁבוּ אֲבוֹתֵיכֶם מֵעוֹלָם, תֶּרַח אֲבִי אַבְרָהָם וַאֲבִי נָחוֹר, וַיַּעַבְדוּ אֱלֹהִים אֲחֵרִים. וָאֶקַּח אֶת־אֲבִיכֶם אֶת־אַבְרָהָם מֵעֵבֶר הַנָּהָר וָאוֹלֵךְ אוֹתוֹ בְּכָל־אֶרֶץ כְּנָעַן, וָאַרְבֶּה אֶת־זַרְעוֹ וָאֶתֶּן לוֹ אֶת־יִצְחָק, וָאֶתֵּן לְיִצְחָק אֶת־יַעֲקֹב וְאֶת־עֵשָׂו. וָאֶתֵּן לְעֵשָׂו אֶת־הַר שֵׂעִיר לָרֶשֶׁת אֹתוֹ, וְיַעֲקֹב וּבָנָיו יָרְדוּ מִצְרָיִם.

*And now, God has brought us close to His worship, as it is stated (Joshua 24:2–4):
"Joshua said to the whole people, so said the Lord, God of Israel, 'Over the river did
your ancestors dwell from always, Terach the father of Abraham and the father of
Nachor, and they worshiped other gods. And I took your father, Abraham, from over
the river and I made him walk in all the land of Canaan and I increased his seed and
I gave him Isaac. And I gave to Isaac, Jacob, and Esau; and I gave to Esau, Mount Seir
[in order that he] inherit it; and Jacob and his sons went down to Egypt.'"*

בָּרוּךְ שׁוֹמֵר הַבְטָחָתוֹ לְיִשְׂרָאֵל, בָּרוּךְ הוּא. שֶׁהַקָּדוֹשׁ בָּרוּךְ הוּא חִשַּׁב אֶת־הַקֵּץ,
לַעֲשׂוֹת כְּמוֹ שֶׁאָמַר לְאַבְרָהָם אָבִינוּ בִּבְרִית בֵּין הַבְּתָרִים, שֶׁנֶּאֱמַר: "וַיֹּאמֶר
לְאַבְרָם, יָדֹעַ תֵּדַע כִּי־גֵר יִהְיֶה זַרְעֲךָ בְּאֶרֶץ לֹא לָהֶם, וַעֲבָדוּם וְעִנּוּ אֹתָם אַרְבַּע
מֵאוֹת שָׁנָה. וְגַם אֶת־הַגּוֹי אֲשֶׁר יַעֲבֹדוּ דָּן אָנֹכִי וְאַחֲרֵי־כֵן יֵצְאוּ בִּרְכֻשׁ גָּדוֹל."

*Blessed be the One who keeps His promise to Israel, blessed be He; since the Holy One,
blessed be He, calculated the end [of the exile,] to do as He said to Abraham, our father,
in the Covenant between the Pieces, as it is stated (Genesis 15:13–14): "And He said to
Abram, 'You should surely know that your seed will be a stranger in a land that is not
theirs, and they will enslave them and afflict them four hundred years. And also that nation
for which they shall toil will I judge, and afterwards they will go out with much property.'"*

In Every Generation, Someone
Seeks to Annihilate the Jews

Cover the *matzah*, lift the cup, and say:

וְהִיא שֶׁעָמְדָה לַאֲבוֹתֵינוּ וְלָנוּ. שֶׁלֹּא אֶחָד בִּלְבָד עָמַד עָלֵינוּ לְכַלּוֹתֵנוּ, אֶלָּא שֶׁבְּכָל
דּוֹר וָדוֹר עוֹמְדִים עָלֵינוּ לְכַלּוֹתֵנוּ, וְהַקָּדוֹשׁ בָּרוּךְ הוּא מַצִּילֵנוּ מִיָּדָם.

*And it is this that has stood for our ancestors and for us. Not only one [person or
nation] has arisen to annihilate us, but rather in each generation, they arise to annihilate
us. But the Holy One, blessed be He, rescues us from their hand.*

This is among the central themes of both the Seder and Jewish history.

For Discussion
Is It True That Someone Arises in Every Generation
to Annihilate the Jews?

There are three assertions here.

1. "In every generation . . ."

When I was a child, I remember thinking that I did not agree with what the Rabbis wrote
here. It was the early 1960s, less than twenty years after the Germans had sought to annihilate the Jews. I was certain that, having seen what horrors antisemitism had led to, no leader
or nation would again seek to annihilate us Jews—certainly not in this generation, so soon
after the Nazis. This generation, I believed, would prove what the Rabbis wrote to be wrong.

Then came May 1967, when Egypt did not seek merely to win a war against Israel, but,
as Egypt's president, Gamal Abdel Nasser, declared at the time, "the destruction of Israel."
This goal was echoed by leaders throughout the Arab world. In the words of Iraq's president, Abdul Rahman Arif: "Our goal is clear—to wipe Israel off the map."

I quickly came to realize that I had been naïve; those who wrote this prayer may well have been right. It may be that in every generation, someone does seek to annihilate the Jews.

2. "To annihilate us . . ."

Among the world's many ethnic, religious, and racial bigotries, antisemitism has been and remains unique in that it often seeks total annihilation. Antisemitism is rarely a matter of only disliking Jews. I wish it were. It is often about annihilating them. Of the almost two hundred member states of the United Nations, most have enemies, but no other country has enemies who seek to annihilate it, to wipe it off the map. At the time of this writing, the government of the Islamic Republic of Iran regularly announces that its primary goal is to annihilate Israel. So, the Rabbis were right when they composed this prayer two thousand years ago.

3. "But God rescues us."

The prayer concludes with the promise that "the Holy One, blessed be He, rescues us from their hands." Now, clearly God didn't save millions of Jews in the Holocaust. But neither this prayer nor the Torah ever promised that God would save every persecuted Jew. God saves "us," meaning the Jewish people. And whether one attributes the Jews' survival to God or to something else, the fact is, despite all the attempts to annihilate the Jews, the Jews are still around—something that cannot be said of nearly any other nation from the ancient world. As the eminent writer Walker Percy wrote:

> Why does no one find it remarkable that in most world cities today there are Jews, but not one single Hittite, even though the Hittites had a flourishing civilization while the Jews nearby were a weak and obscure people? When one meets a Jew in New York or New Orleans or Paris or Melbourne, it is remarkable that no one considers the event remarkable. What are they doing here? But it is even more remarkable to wonder, if there are Jews here, why are there not Hittites here? Where are the Hittites? Show me one Hittite in New York City.

Put down the cup of wine, uncover the *matzot*, and say:

צֵא וּלְמַד מַה בִּקֵּשׁ לָבָן הָאֲרַמִּי לַעֲשׂוֹת לְיַעֲקֹב אָבִינוּ: שֶׁפַּרְעֹה לֹא גָזַר אֶלָּא עַל הַזְּכָרִים, וְלָבָן בִּקֵּשׁ לַעֲקֹר אֶת־הַכֹּל. שֶׁנֶּאֱמַר: אֲרַמִּי אֹבֵד אָבִי, וַיֵּרֶד מִצְרַיְמָה וַיָּגָר שָׁם בִּמְתֵי מְעָט, וַיְהִי שָׁם לְגוֹי גָּדוֹל, עָצוּם וָרָב.

Go out and learn what Laban the Aramean sought to do to Jacob, our father; since Pharaoh only decreed [the death sentence] on the males but Laban sought to uproot the whole [people]. As it is stated (Deuteronomy 26:5), "An Aramean was destroying my father and he went down to Egypt, and he resided there with a small number and there he became a nation, great, powerful and numerous."

וַיֵּרֶד מִצְרַיְמָה – אָנוּס עַל פִּי הַדִּבּוּר. וַיָּגָר שָׁם. מְלַמֵּד שֶׁלֹּא יָרַד יַעֲקֹב אָבִינוּ לְהִשְׁתַּקֵּעַ בְּמִצְרַיִם אֶלָּא לָגוּר שָׁם, שֶׁנֶּאֱמַר: וַיֹּאמְרוּ אֶל־פַּרְעֹה, לָגוּר בָּאָרֶץ בָּאנוּ, כִּי אֵין מִרְעֶה לַצֹּאן אֲשֶׁר לַעֲבָדֶיךָ, כִּי כָבֵד הָרָעָב בְּאֶרֶץ כְּנָעַן. וְעַתָּה יֵשְׁבוּ־נָא עֲבָדֶיךָ בְּאֶרֶץ גֹּשֶׁן.

"And he went down to Egypt"—helpless on account of the word [in which God told Abraham that his descendants would have to go into exile]. "And he resided there"— [this] teaches that Jacob, our father, didn't go down to settle in Egypt, but rather [only] to reside there, as it is stated (Genesis 47:4), "And they said to Pharaoh, 'We have come to reside in the land, since there is not enough pasture for your servant's flocks, since the famine is heavy in the land of Canaan, and now please grant that your servants should dwell in the Land of Goshen.'"

בִּמְתֵי מְעָט. כְּמָה שֶׁנֶּאֱמַר: בְּשִׁבְעִים נֶפֶשׁ יָרְדוּ אֲבוֹתֶיךָ מִצְרַיְמָה, וְעַתָּה שָׂמְךָ ה' אֱלֹהֶיךָ כְּכוֹכְבֵי הַשָּׁמַיִם לָרֹב.

"As a small number"—as it is stated (Deuteronomy 10:22), "With seventy souls did your ancestors come down to Egypt, and now the Lord your God has made you as numerous as the stars of the sky."

וַיְהִי שָׁם לְגוֹי. מְלַמֵּד שֶׁהָיוּ יִשְׂרָאֵל מְצֻיָּנִים שָׁם. גָּדוֹל עָצוּם – כְּמָה שֶׁנֶּאֱמַר: וּבְנֵי יִשְׂרָאֵל פָּרוּ וַיִּשְׁרְצוּ וַיִּרְבּוּ וַיַּעַצְמוּ בִּמְאֹד מְאֹד, וַתִּמָּלֵא הָאָרֶץ אֹתָם.

"And he became there a nation"—[this] teaches that Israel [became] distinguishable there. "Great, powerful"—as it is stated (Exodus 1:7): "And the Children of Israel multiplied and swarmed and grew numerous and strong, most exceedingly, and the land was filled with them."

Although the Israelites were granted permission to live only in the area of Egypt known as Goshen (Genesis 45:10), in the eyes of Pharaoh and the Egyptians, "the land was filled with them." Throughout history, antisemites—and even many non-Jews sympathetic to Jews—often wildly overstated the number of Jews in their country.

I remember an incident in my early years of lecturing that perfectly illustrates this point. A non-Jewish woman seated next me on a flight to Louisville, Kentucky, asked me what brought me to her city. I told her I was going to speak to the Louisville Jewish community. As the conversation continued on the subject of Jews, it became apparent that this woman thought there were far more Jews in Kentucky than there actually were. So, I decided to ask her how many Jews she thought lived in the United States. After noting that there were then about 215 million Americans, I asked her how many of them she thought were Jews. She pondered the question for a moment and responded, "About 50 million." Obviously startled when I told her there were 6 million Jews in America, she said, "I guess they must all live in Kentucky."

As of this writing, there are about 14 million Jews in a world population approaching 8 billion. That means that Jews comprise fewer than 2 out of 1,000 people in the world. But few people would guess this because Jewish influence has always been so disproportionate to the size of the Jewish population. And the reason for that influence is ultimately the values bequeathed by the Torah and the later Judaism that emanated from it. Given the tiny number of Jews, there is no other explanation.

וָרָב. כְּמָה שֶׁנֶּאֱמַר: רְבָבָה כְּצֶמַח הַשָּׂדֶה נְתַתִּיךְ, וַתִּרְבִּי וַתִּגְדְּלִי וַתָּבֹאִי בַּעֲדִי עֲדָיִים, שָׁדַיִם נָכֹנוּ וּשְׂעָרֵךְ צִמֵּחַ, וְאַתְּ עֵרֹם וְעֶרְיָה. וָאֶעֱבֹר עָלַיִךְ וָאֶרְאֵךְ מִתְבּוֹסֶסֶת בְּדָמָיִךְ, וָאֹמַר לָךְ בְּדָמַיִךְ חֲיִי, וָאֹמַר לָךְ בְּדָמַיִךְ חֲיִי.

"And numerous"—as it is stated (Ezekiel 16:7): "I have given you to be numerous as the vegetation of the field, and you increased and grew and became highly ornamented, your breasts were set and your hair grew, but you were naked and barren. And I passed over you and saw you downtrodden in your blood and I said to you: 'Through your blood shall you live!' And I said to you: 'Through your blood shall you live!'"

For Discussion
Is There Such a Thing as Collective Guilt?
The Guilt of the Egyptian People

וַיָּרֵעוּ אֹתָנוּ הַמִּצְרִים וַיְעַנּוּנוּ, וַיִּתְּנוּ עָלֵינוּ עֲבֹדָה קָשָׁה. וַיָּרֵעוּ אֹתָנוּ הַמִּצְרִים — כְּמָה שֶׁנֶּאֱמַר: הָבָה נִתְחַכְּמָה לוֹ פֶּן יִרְבֶּה, וְהָיָה כִּי תִקְרֶאנָה מִלְחָמָה וְנוֹסַף גַּם הוּא עַל שֹׂנְאֵינוּ וְנִלְחַם־בָּנוּ, וְעָלָה מִן־הָאָרֶץ.

"And the Egyptians did bad to us" (Deuteronomy 26:6)—as it is stated (Exodus 1:10): "Let us be wise towards him, lest he multiply and it will be that when war is called, he too will join with our enemies and fight against us and go up from the land."

וַיְעַנּוּנוּ. כְּמָה שֶׁנֶּאֱמַר: וַיָּשִׂימוּ עָלָיו שָׂרֵי מִסִּים לְמַעַן עַנֹּתוֹ בְּסִבְלֹתָם. וַיִּבֶן עָרֵי מִסְכְּנוֹת לְפַרְעֹה. אֶת־פִּתֹם וְאֶת־רַעַמְסֵס. וַיִּתְּנוּ עָלֵינוּ עֲבֹדָה קָשָׁה. כְּמָה שֶׁנֶּאֱמַר: וַיַּעֲבִדוּ מִצְרַיִם אֶת־בְּנֵי יִשְׂרָאֵל בְּפָרֶךְ.

"And afflicted us"—as it is stated (Exodus 1:11): "And they placed upon him leaders over the work-tax in order to afflict them with their burdens; and they built storage cities, Pithom and Ra'amses." "And put upon us hard work"—as it is stated (Exodus 1:13): "And they enslaved the children of Israel with breaking work."

The Torah emphasizes the collective guilt of the Egyptians. It was Pharaoh who initiated the slavery and annihilation campaign, but the Egyptian people executed it. Individuals initiate mass evil, but they need the collaboration of many people to carry it out. This explains the collective national punishments the Egyptian people would experience.

The last verse of the first chapter of Exodus (Exodus 1:22) reads: "And Pharaoh ordered *all* his people saying, 'Every boy that is born you shall throw into the river . . .'" [emphasis added].

The Torah makes clear that when it comes to individual crimes, punishment is to be inflicted only on the responsible individual. If a member of a family or clan murders a member of another family or clan, it is expressly forbidden to punish the murderer's family or clan (Leviticus 24:17, 19–20). The restriction of punishment to the guilty party is one of the great moral advances of the Torah. Yet another Torah innovation is found in the much-misunderstood Torah law of an "eye for an eye . . . a life for a life." Every punishment must be equivalent to the crime—not more—and, as noted, must be inflicted only on the perpetrator—not on his family. All the other punishments, with the exception of capital punishment for murder, are financial, not physical (see *The Rational Bible* commentary to Exodus 21:24–25).

But when it comes to mass evil committed by a nation, there can indeed be collective guilt. We cannot deny national evil just because not every member of a nation is guilty.

Take slavery in America. The whole American nation paid a terrible price—as the whole Egyptian nation did—because of the national crime of African slavery. America fought its Civil War because of slavery—a war in which as many Americans died as in all the other American wars combined (a list that includes World Wars I and II, the Korean War, and the Vietnam War). Over 700,000 Americans died, a particularly striking number given that America's population in 1860 was only 31 million.

As in all wars, many of those most deserving of punishment got away with their crimes. In the case of American slavery, for example, the slave kidnappers and traders (who deserved the death penalty, according to Exodus 21:16) were long dead by the time of the war their actions helped bring about, yet 700,000 Americans died because of those actions. The only perfect justice is in the world to come.

Statements on slavery by two of America's greatest presidents affirm the notion of collective guilt. Thomas Jefferson, the third American president and the author of America's Declaration of Independence, warned that Americans would one day collectively pay for the sin of slavery: "I tremble for my country when I reflect that God is just: that his justice cannot sleep forever." (Jefferson acknowledged the evil of slavery even though he was a slave owner.)

During the American Civil War, Abraham Lincoln, too, affirmed America's collective guilt for slavery: "Fondly do we hope, fervently do we pray, that this mighty scourge of war may speedily pass away. Yet, if God wills that it continue until . . . every drop of blood drawn with the lash shall be paid by another drawn with the sword, as was said three thousand years ago, so it must be said, 'The judgments of the Lord are true and righteous altogether'" (Psalm 19:10).

To deny this, Lincoln told friends a week later, "is to deny that there is a God governing the world." Lincoln knew his Bible. While he did not regularly attend church, he constantly studied the Bible. As he put it, "In regard to this Great Book, I have but to say, it is the best gift God has given to man. . . . But for it we could not know right from wrong."

Slavery was a universally practiced evil (including among indigenous peoples and in Africa). But many of the crimes of Germany during World War II were unique. And given most Germans' knowledge of and/or active support for Hitler's invasions of countries and bombings of civilian centers, and their active or tacit support for slave labor and mass deportations of Jews (even if many Germans did not know these people would be murdered), the Western democracies did not deem it immoral to bomb German cities. There was a general sense that the German people, not just a handful of Nazis, were responsible for Nazi evil.

Among the first orders General Dwight D. Eisenhower, the head of the Allied war effort, issued after victory over Germany was a decree ordering local German populations to view the horrors committed in the concentration and death camps in their vicinity, and to provide a proper burial for the mounds of corpses abandoned by Nazi guards when they fled the camps as the Allied armies approached. Eisenhower apparently believed Germans in general, not just German leaders, were responsible for the unfathomable crimes committed by their country.

You don't need a great number of truly evil people for massive evil to be committed. You only need a paucity of courageous people.

Most Egyptians were not as evil as Pharaoh, just as most Germans were not as evil as Hitler. There are relatively few truly evil people in the world. However, you don't need a great number of truly evil people for massive evil to be committed. You only need a paucity of courageous people. Courage is the rarest of all the good traits. There are many more kind and honest people than courageous people. Unfortunately, in the battle against evil, all the good traits in the world amount to little when not accompanied by courage. (Of course, the reference is to courage in the service of good; there is ample courage in the service of evil.)

Perhaps to teach the importance of courage in the service of good, the Torah depicts this very trait immediately following these verses (Exodus 1:15–21) in the story of the two midwives Shifrah and Puah, who refused to follow Pharaoh's orders to kill Israelite boys.

For Discussion
Is It Possible to Reconcile a Good God with Unjust Suffering?

וַנִּצְעַק אֶל־ה' אֱלֹהֵי אֲבֹתֵינוּ, וַיִּשְׁמַע ה' אֶת־קֹלֵנוּ, וַיַּרְא אֶת־עָנְיֵנוּ וְאֶת עֲמָלֵנוּ וְאֶת לַחֲצֵנוּ.

"And we cried out to the Lord, the God of our ancestors, and the Lord heard our voice, and He saw our affliction, and our toil and our duress" (Deuteronomy 26:7).

וַנִּצְעַק אֶל־ה' אֱלֹהֵי אֲבֹתֵינוּ – כְּמָה שֶׁנֶּאֱמַר: וַיְהִי בַיָּמִים הָרַבִּים הָהֵם וַיָּמָת מֶלֶךְ מִצְרַיִם, וַיֵּאָנְחוּ בְנֵי־יִשְׂרָאֵל מִן־הָעֲבוֹדָה וַיִּזְעָקוּ, וַתַּעַל שַׁוְעָתָם אֶל־הָאֱלֹהִים מִן הָעֲבֹדָה.

"And we cried out to the Lord, the God of our ancestors"—as it is stated (Exodus 2:23):
"And it was in those great days that the king of Egypt died and the Children of Israel sighed from the work and yelled out, and their supplication went up to God from the work."

וַיִּשְׁמַע ה' אֶת קֹלֵנוּ. כְּמָה שֶׁנֶּאֱמַר: וַיִּשְׁמַע אֱלֹהִים אֶת־נַאֲקָתָם, וַיִּזְכֹּר אֱלֹהִים אֶת־בְּרִיתוֹ אֶת־אַבְרָהָם, אֶת־יִצְחָק וְאֶת־יַעֲקֹב.

"And the Lord heard our voice"—as it is stated (Exodus 2:24): "And God heard their groans and God remembered His covenant with Abraham and with Isaac and with Jacob."

What does the Torah mean when it says "and God remembered"? Did God suddenly recall His covenant with Abraham, Isaac, and Jacob and only then decide to take the Israelites out of Egypt? The answer is that when the Torah describes God as "remembering," it does not mean the same as humans' remembering. Humans forget and then remember. God does not forget. "God remembers" means God has decided to act.

Why did God decide at that moment and not sooner?

The answer is that God works according to His own inscrutable timetable. From our perspective, God rarely steps in early enough. Indeed, when it comes to rescuing the just from the unjust, much of the time God doesn't seem to act at all.

Why not?

To such questions, we have no definitive answers. Ever since the biblical Book of Job, people have asked why God allows the just to suffer. One can only conclude, as the medieval Hebrew saying goes, "If I *knew* God, I'd *be* God" (*lu yidativ hayitiv*).

However, there are three plausible explanations:

First, as noted above, if God always intervened to stop evil, human beings would not have free will. Morally speaking, we would be robots.

Second, the only possible answer to the problem of unjust suffering is that there is justice in an afterlife. If God is just, it is axiomatic there is an afterlife. (See the discussion about the afterlife on pages 37–39.)

Third, I have always been moved by an argument put forward by the late American rabbi Milton Steinberg: The believer has to account for the existence of one thing—unjust suffering. The atheist has to account for the existence of everything else.

Since Steinberg made his argument, science has affirmed its legitimacy. When Rabbi Steinberg first offered his argument, most scientists believed that the atheist could indeed explain the existence of "everything else" (the material universe). They believed the universe had always existed. Therefore, no explanation for its existence was required. Science has since shown that the universe had a beginning in the form of a massive explosion—an event dubbed "the Big Bang."

> *If God is just, it is axiomatic there is an afterlife.*

Another way of expressing the Steinberg argument was made a half-century before Steinberg by the great English thinker G. K. Chesterton: "The riddles of God are more satisfying than the solutions of man."

For Discussion
Is God Good?

To believe God exists demands no leap of faith. The arguments for the existence of a Creator as the source of design and intelligence are more rational than arguments that life arose from non-life, intelligence arose from non-intelligence, and the entire material universe arose by itself.

What does demand some leap of faith is the belief that God is good. Given the amount of unjust suffering, natural and man-made, that vast numbers of human beings have endured, it is not axiomatic that God is good. Nevertheless, I do believe God is good, and reason alone argues for that proposition.

Would a God who was not good create creatures who knew and did good, who felt and displayed compassion? Would a God who was not good make so much that is beautiful both in the world and in the human being? Is there anyone at this Seder who has not experienced immense good and immense joy? Would a God who was not good have made that possible? Moreover, the problem of unjust suffering is a problem only if one posits there is a good God.

The fact is that the answer to the problem of theodicy—how to reconcile a good God with suffering and evil—is not available to us. But it does not strike me as probable that the Creator created the world in order that His creatures suffer. A God who is either indifferent to all suffering or, worse, who actually revels in it does not seem likely. It would mean, among other things, that God made beings who are vastly morally superior to Him. Moreover, why would human beings have a conscience if the Creator of human beings had no interest in goodness?

The problem of unjust suffering is a problem only if one posits there is a good God.

Additionally, for many reasons (see "Arguments for the Divinity of the Torah" below), it is inconceivable to me that men (and/or women) authored the Torah. There is nothing in history morally or intellectually comparable to the Torah. And this Torah is filled with too much goodness, too much innovative moral teaching, to substantiate the idea that the Creator of the world and of the Torah is a bad God.

For Discussion

1. Do you believe God is good?
2. Do you love God?
3. Do you believe God loves you?

For Discussion
Is the Torah Divine or Man-Made?
Arguments for the Divinity of the Torah

1. The Torah is virtually as different from everything that preceded it as Creation was from what preceded it. In other words, both Creation and the Torah came, as it were, *ex nihilo* (out of nothing). And just as *creatio ex nihilo* argues for a Divine Creator, so the

creation of the Torah argues for a Divine Author. Either moral and intellectual supermen are the source of the Torah, or God is.

2. The God of the Torah is the first universal god in history. All other gods were national or ethnic gods.

3. For the first time in history, God is moral, not capricious. Therefore, for the first time, man can argue with this deity, which is precisely what the first Jew, Abraham, did when he challenged God's justice: "Shall not the judge of all the earth deal justly?" (Genesis 18:25).

4. This God, unlike other gods, judges all nations and individuals—and judges them by the same moral standard.

5. The God of the Torah, unlike other gods, is completely de-sexualized. He does not procreate with other gods or with humans. Nor was He born.

6. The God of the Torah loves human beings and wants to be loved. For the first time in any recorded literature, people were instructed not just to fear but to love their God.

7. The God of the Torah is invisible and incorporeal.

8. The God of the Torah is not part of nature, as all other gods were. He is the creator of nature, not part of it.

These characteristics were unique to the God introduced by the Torah. The idea that people made all this up—in the late Bronze Age, no less—is less rationally compelling than the idea that God revealed it.

9. The Torah is the first text we know of that describes the creation of woman.

10. In the major religious texts of other religions, the people of those religions are described positively. In the Torah, the Jews are constantly described in negative terms. As previously argued, it is almost inconceivable that Jews would have depicted their own people as negatively as the Torah depicts them.

11. In contrast, and equally unexpectedly, the Torah frequently depicts non-Jews in positive terms—often as heroes. Noah was a not a Jew, yet he is described as a *tzaddik*, the highest Torah appellation for a righteous person. The non-Israelite midwives who resisted Pharaoh's order to kill the Israelite male infants are presented as heroes. And despite Midrashic claims to the contrary, the text seems clear that Shifrah and Puah were not Israelites.[9] (For the record, the great medieval philosopher Don Isaac Abarbanel also believed the midwives were not Israelites.) Caleb, the hero of the spies story and the one spy (other than Joshua) to give a favorable report about the Israelites being able to conquer Canaan, was not an ethnic Israelite. Jethro, Moses's father-in-law and mentor, was a Midianite. And, of course, Moses's life was saved by the daughter of Pharaoh. Given the Jews' (justified) animosity toward the Egyptians, why would a Jew later make up such a story?

12. The number of later Torah and other Jewish laws violated by the patriarchs, matriarchs, and Joseph strongly argues for the authenticity of the text and against the notion that later Jews wrote it. Had later Jews written it, they would almost certainly not have described practices of the patriarchs that violated later Torah and rabbinic laws. For example, Abraham apparently served meat and milk at the same meal (Genesis 18:7–8); Moses's father married his aunt (Exodus 6:20), in violation of Leviticus 18:14; and Joseph practiced divination (Genesis 44:5 and 15), in violation of Deuteronomy 18:10–11.

13. The Torah's morality was a unique innovation. Its most frequently repeated law is to love the stranger. What other religious text in the world had such an injunction? The choosing of Abraham's seed—the Hebrews, Israelites, Jews—was done so this people would be a blessing to all the nations of the world. Where else was such a notion ever conceived? "Love your neighbor as yourself" comes from the Torah. Virtually every ancient people had a flood narrative, but only in the Torah's flood story did the God save the hero because he was the most righteous person in his time—rather than, for example, the handsomest or strongest. And, for the first time in history, the universal practice of human sacrifice was outlawed.

14. The Torah's profundity about life is unmatched by any other literature. The rest of the Bible is a close second, but it is all based on the Torah. That is why there are more Bible commentaries than commentaries on any other literature. That's why even nonreligious figures throughout history studied and revered it more than any other literature. In addition to Abraham Lincoln, the original American founders, Benjamin Franklin and Thomas Jefferson, neither of whom was religious, so revered the Bible that they designed a Great Seal of the United States which depicted the Israelites leaving Egypt. The inscription on the most important symbol of the American Revolution, the Liberty Bell, is a verse from the Torah (Leviticus 25:10). The insignia of Yale University contains the Hebrew words *Urim v'Tummim*, the words the Torah instructed the Israelites to inscribe on the breastplate of the High Priest in Jerusalem.

The Torah, along with the rest of the Bible, is the basis of Western civilization. It is difficult to imagine this civilization surviving the neglect and rejection of the book that made the civilization possible.

I am well aware of the moral arguments against divine authorship, such as the Torah's not completely outlawing slavery, the law prescribing the stoning of a rebellious son, various sexual prohibitions, the execution of a man who publicly violated Shabbat, the "eye for an eye" law, scientific arguments against it, and the Torah's alleged inconsistencies. I believe there are rational and moral responses to them. (On the few occasions

I found problems not having to do with morality that I could not explain, I acknowledge that fact.) But considering the Torah's unique greatness, I no more regard the things I cannot explain as invalidating God as the ultimate author of the Torah than I regard the things I cannot explain about the world (such as unjust suffering or seeming "mistakes" in the design of the human body) as invalidating God as the Creator.

My belief in and love for the Torah are so great that I came to realize that I do not believe in the Torah because I believe in God; I believe in God because I believe in the Torah.

For Discussion
How Important Is Divine Authorship of the Torah?

Many Jews and others do not understand why the question of whether the Torah is from God or man is so important.

I will offer the first reason by way of a personal illustration.

In my teens and early twenties, I had some tension with my parents. This is hardly worth mentioning, because tension with parents—especially in one's younger years—is the norm. I mention it to make a crucial point about the Torah and morality. No matter how distant I

I do not believe in the Torah because I believe in God; I believe in God because I believe in the Torah.

felt from my parents, I always honored them and treated them with respect. For example, from the day I left my parents' home at the age of twenty-one until my mother died thirty-nine years later and my father forty-six years later, I called them every week.

I did so, at least in my early years, for one reason: I believed that God had commanded me—yes, me (the Ten Commandments are all in the singular)—to honor my father and mother. It is incontestable that people are more likely to do something (good or evil) if they believe God commanded them to do so. Remove God from the Ten Commandments, and you have nothing more than ten suggestions.

A second reason for the importance of the divinity of the Torah is that if human beings wrote the Torah, human beings can change it—or ignore it. People change or ignore what other people write. Jews who do not regard the Torah as divine may end up rejecting some fundamental Torah principles. To cite one contemporary example, many Jews (and non-Jews) do not consider the commandment "Honor your father and mother" to be binding. Thus, a great number of adult children have severed contact with their mother and/or father.

If you regard the Torah as a collection of ancient human documents, what difference does this or anything else the Torah says make? Why is one compelled to honor any of its contents? Those who believe God commands them to honor their parents are probably considerably less likely to mistreat a parent with whom they are annoyed or even angry.

A third reason belief in the divinity of the Torah is vital is that it enabled Jews to make major sacrifices when it came to Torah principles. Torah-believing Jews sacrificed incomes so as not to work on Shabbat, and even sacrificed their lives because they believed the Torah is from God. This gave them the strength to resist converting to other religions when threatened with death for not converting (a threat often made and carried out by the medieval Crusaders).

Finally, Jewish survival depends on Jews' believing in a divine text. The Jewish people would not have survived for thousands of years without belief that the source of the Torah is divine. Most of the descendants of Jews living outside of Israel who do not believe in the divinity of the Torah—or, at the very least, the Ten Commandments—will eventually assimilate.

Questions for Further Discussion

1. If you don't believe God revealed His will in the Torah, how do you know what God wants of you?

2. If not God, to whom are you morally accountable?

3. Do you think the Ten Commandments are the most important moral code ever devised? If not, what is?

4. Do you believe God will judge you and reward or punish you—or anyone else—after you die?

וַיַּרְא אֶת־עָנְיֵנוּ. זוֹ פְּרִישׁוּת דֶּרֶךְ אֶרֶץ, כְּמָה שֶׁנֶּאֱמַר: וַיַּרְא אֱלֹהִים אֶת בְּנֵי־יִשְׂרָאֵל וַיֵּדַע אֱלֹהִים.

"And He saw our affliction"—[refers to] the separation from the way of the world, as it is stated (Exodus 2:25): "And God saw the Children of Israel and God knew."

וְאֶת־עֲמָלֵנוּ. אֵלוּ הַבָּנִים. כְּמָה שֶׁנֶּאֱמַר: כָּל־הַבֵּן הַיִּלּוֹד הַיְאֹרָה תַּשְׁלִיכֻהוּ וְכָל־הַבַּת תְּחַיּוּן.

"And our toil"—[refers to the killing of] the sons, as it is stated (Exodus 1:22): "Every boy that is born, throw him into the Nile and every girl you shall keep alive."

וְאֶת לַחֲצֵנוּ. זֶו הַדְּחַק, כְּמָה שֶׁנֶּאֱמַר: וְגַם־רָאִיתִי אֶת־הַלַּחַץ אֲשֶׁר מִצְרַיִם לֹחֲצִים אֹתָם.

"And our duress"—[refers to] the pressure, as it is stated (Exodus 3:9): "And I also saw the duress that the Egyptians are applying on them."

וַיּוֹצִאֵנוּ ה' מִמִּצְרַיִם בְּיָד חֲזָקָה, וּבִזְרֹעַ נְטוּיָה, וּבְמֹרָא גָּדֹל, וּבְאֹתוֹת וּבְמֹפְתִים.

"And the Lord took us out of Egypt with a strong hand and with an outstretched forearm and with great awe and with signs and with wonders" (Deuteronomy 26:8).

God Alone—No Angel,
No Human—Killed the Firstborn

וַיּוֹצִאֵנוּ ה' מִמִּצְרָיִם. לֹא עַל־יְדֵי מַלְאָךְ, וְלֹא עַל־יְדֵי שָׂרָף, וְלֹא עַל־יְדֵי שָׁלִיחַ, אֶלָּא הַקָּדוֹשׁ בָּרוּךְ הוּא בִּכְבוֹדוֹ וּבְעַצְמוֹ. שֶׁנֶּאֱמַר: וְעָבַרְתִּי בְאֶרֶץ מִצְרַיִם בַּלַּיְלָה הַזֶּה, וְהִכֵּיתִי כָל־בְּכוֹר בְּאֶרֶץ מִצְרַיִם מֵאָדָם וְעַד בְּהֵמָה, וּבְכָל אֱלֹהֵי מִצְרַיִם אֶעֱשֶׂה שְׁפָטִים. אֲנִי ה'.

"And the Lord took us out of Egypt"—not through an angel and not through a seraph and not through a messenger, but [directly by] the Holy One, blessed be He, Himself, as it is stated (Exodus 12:12): "And I will pass through the Land of Egypt on that night and I will smite every firstborn in the Land of Egypt, from men to animals; and against all the gods of Egypt, I will make judgments, I am the Lord."

The Torah emphasizes that God Himself—not an angel, not a seraph (a high-ranking angel), not a messenger (Moses, for example), and not one Jew—killed the firstborn in Egypt. The Torah implicitly acknowledges the moral problem of the killing of the firstborn, and therefore makes clear that God alone undertook their execution.

For Discussion
The Essence of Judaism: The Denial of False Gods

וְעָבַרְתִּי בְאֶרֶץ מִצְרַיִם בַּלַּיְלָה הַזֶּה – אֲנִי וְלֹא מַלְאָךְ; וְהִכֵּיתִי כָל בְּכוֹר בְּאֶרֶץ־מִצְרָיִם. אֲנִי וְלֹא שָׂרָף; וּבְכָל־אֱלֹהֵי מִצְרַיִם אֶעֱשֶׂה שְׁפָטִים. אֲנִי וְלֹא הַשָּׁלִיחַ; אֲנִי ה'. אֲנִי הוּא וְלֹא אַחֵר.

"And I will pass through the Land of Egypt"—I and not an angel. "And I will smite every firstborn"—I and not a seraph. "And against all the gods of Egypt, I will make judgments." I and not a messenger. "I am the Lord"—I am He and there is no other.

This statement—"against all the gods of Egypt, I will make judgments"—is of enormous importance. Each of the Ten Plagues was directed against a god of Egypt. In order for the Israelites to accept God, they first had to be convinced that the gods of Egypt were powerless, and therefore not gods. The road to God and to a good world is possible only when all false gods are rejected.

The ten plagues constitute a partial list of Egyptian gods against which the plagues were directed. Note that all were nature-gods. The Torah's God is the creator of nature, not part of it.

- First plague (water turned to blood): the gods attached to the Nile River.
- Second plague (frogs): the frog god and goddess.
- Third plague (lice): the earth god: "Hold out your rod and strike the dust of the earth, and it shall turn to lice throughout the land of Egypt."
- Fourth plague (flies/insects): the fly-god and/or the beetle god.
- Fifth plague (diseased cattle): gods associated with bulls and cows.
- Sixth plague (boils): gods of healing.
- Seventh plague (hail): gods of the sky, atmosphere, and agriculture.
- Eighth plague (locusts): the gods who protected against locusts and human disease.
- Ninth plague (darkness): the sun god and moon god.
- Tenth plague (deaths of firstborn): all of Egypt's gods, including the man-god Pharaoh, whose first-born son was killed; a response to the mass killing of the Hebrews' sons.

For Discussion
The False Gods of Our Time

The need to deny false gods is as relevant today as it was in ancient Egypt. And the list of false gods is at least as long. The only difference between our gods and those of the ancients is that ours are not physical. In fact, a case can be made for this commandment's being the most important of the Ten Commandments. The Talmud, the most significant Jewish text after the Bible, actually says as much: "Whoever denies idolatry is like one who acknowledges the entire Torah."[10]

Nearly two thousand years later, the philosopher and psychoanalyst Erich Fromm—who called himself a "radical humanist"—said the same thing. Fromm's book *You Shall*

Be as Gods was largely devoted to rejecting false gods, which, he argued, should be the most important goal of mankind.[11] Both human progress and the making of a good world are dependent on the rejection of false gods. This commandment is therefore not primarily a ban on worshiping idols—the word "gods," not "idols," is used (idol-worship is specifically prohibited in the next commandment).

A false god is anything people worship other than the God of the Ten Commandments. Here are seven examples:[12]

Education
Art
Love
Reason
Money
Intelligence
Science

The reader will note that (except for money) each of these things is properly regarded as among humanity's highest ideals and values. However, as demonstrated at great length in *The Rational Bible* commentaries on Exodus and Deuteronomy, when God and His commandments are removed from these values, they can, and often do, become vehicles to moral chaos and ultimately to evil.

To cite just one example—education—many of the best-educated people in Germany supported Hitler and the Nazis. Professor Peter Merkl of the University of California at Santa Barbara studied 581 Nazis and found that Germans with a high school education "or even university study" (at a time when a much smaller percentage of the population attended university) were more likely to be antisemitic than those with less education.[13]

As regards support for Stalin and communism, the record is even worse. Professor George Watson of Cambridge University wrote: "The published evidence alone demonstrates that many Western intellectuals in the age of Stalin believed in extermination in the sense of wanting it to happen."[14]

At the time of this writing, the most anti-Israel individuals and groups are to be found disproportionately among the best-educated. These people learned to hate Israel—and even to support movements for Israel's extinction—at university.[15]

Questions for Further Discussion

1. Would you rather your children be secular or even non-believers and attend Harvard or some other prestigious university, or be religiously committed and attend a non-prestigious university?

2. Ask your children (of any age): "What do you think I most want you to be—happy, successful, smart, or good?" Make sure they understand that you are not asking what they most want to be, but what they think you most want them to be.

How do you think they would respond? How would you want them to respond? And if you did ask them, how did they respond?

Finally, ask them which one they most want to be.

For Discussion
Do All Those Who Believe in God Believe in the Same God?

The Torah repeatedly makes clear that the worship of God means following God's moral dictates. Obeying God's commands is what worshiping God means.

Let us now turn to the related but broader question of what belief in God means.

Vast numbers of people—both within and outside of religion—say they believe in God. But if belief in God means living according to God's moral dictates, how many people actually believe in God, even allowing for the inevitable transgressions that all human beings, including the finest, will occasionally engage in?

Who would have the audacity to claim that they believed in God? If they examine the way they lived, who would dare say that?
—Jordan Peterson

This question was answered powerfully by a prominent contemporary thinker, Jordan Peterson, a professor of psychology at the University of Toronto, when I asked him in a public dialogue we engaged in if he believed in God. This was his answer:

> Who would have the audacity to claim that they believed in God? If they examine the way they lived, who would dare say that? . . . To face things courageously and to tell the truth, to speak the truth and to act it out, that's what it means to believe. That's what it means. It doesn't mean to state it. It means to act it out. And unless you act it out, you should be very careful about claiming it [belief]. And so, I've

never been comfortable saying anything other than I try to act as if God exists because God only knows what you'd be if you truly believed.

The issue of who really believes in God is related to another: Do all people who believe in God believe in the same god? More specifically, do they all believe in the God the Torah introduced to the world? The answer is no.

This question is so important because the God of the Torah (and the rest of the Bible) is often blamed by anti-religious people for any terrible actions committed by anyone who claims to believe in God. After all, even Hitler claimed a belief in God, and the anti-religious often cite this fact in response to those of us who argue for the moral necessity of God. But Hitler did not believe in the God of the Bible. Indeed, the Nazis promulgated the doctrine of "Aryan Christianity," Christianity purged of its Jewish elements, such as the Old Testament. He used the same word as the Bible—"God"—but his "God" and the God of the Bible had nothing in common.

When Jews, Christians, or Muslims—let alone people who identify with no specific religion—say, "I believe in God," they are not necessarily talking about the same God. In fact, the statement "I believe in God" tells us nothing about a person's beliefs, values, or the god in whom the person believes. To cite an obvious example, a god in whose name believers cut innocent people's throats, behead them, burn them alive, and rape girls and women—as is being done at the time of this writing by Islamist terrorists in the name of Allah (Arabic for "God")—cannot be the same god as the God of the Torah. The God of the Torah gave the Ten Commandments, commanded His people to "love the stranger," and demanded holy and ethical conduct at all times. Likewise, those Christians who, in the Middle Ages, slaughtered entire Jewish communities in the name of Christ also clearly did not believe in the God of the Bible, as virtually every Christian today would acknowledge. Nor were they instructed to commit their atrocities by either the Old or the New Testament. Of course, there have also been Jews who supported evil—such as those who supported Stalin (many of the leading spies who gave Stalin the secrets to making a nuclear bomb were Jews)—but they did not do so in the name of God. Indeed, they were proud atheists.

Yet, there are many people who argue that those who say they believe in God believe in the same god. Why do they make this argument? Because all too often they have an anti-religious agenda.

So, then, how are we to know whether any two people who say they believe in God believe in the same God, the God of the Torah?

We can find out by asking three questions:

1. Do you believe in the God introduced to the world by the Jews and their Bible—the God known as the "God of Israel"?

Before responding, some people might need to have the term defined. The "God of Israel" is the God introduced to the world by the Jews and their Bible. This is the God Who created the world, Who revealed Himself to the Jews, and Who made His moral will known through the Ten Commandments, the rest of the Torah, and the Hebrew prophets.

2. Does the god you believe in judge the moral behavior of every human being—and by the same moral standard?

There are many people who say they believe in God, but not in a God who judges people's actions. These people generally affirm no specific religion. They say God is "a personal thing," or "God is within me." But if God is only a personal thing or only within them, who outside of them will judge them? They can be fine people. But the question is not whether there are any good people who do not believe in the God of the Torah. Of course there are. The question is whether all people who say they believe in God believe in the same God, the God introduced by the Torah.

People who believe in a god who does not morally judge people do not believe in the God of the Torah, because they believe in a god who is ultimately indifferent to the moral behavior of human beings. And such a god is so different from the God of the Torah that these people should use a word other than "God."

Now, one might argue Islamist terrorists also believe in a judging God, as did Tomas de Torquemada, the infamous Catholic head of the Spanish Inquisition. But such individuals believe God judges people solely by their faith, not by their moral behavior, and that is not the God of the Torah.

It needs to be emphasized that one need not be a Jew—or a Christian, or a member of any faith—to believe in the God of the Torah. The great Benjamin Franklin, one of America's founders, was one such example. He did not affirm the Christian Trinity, and he was not a Jew. But he believed in the God introduced by the Hebrew Bible, in its moral teachings, and that this God morally judges all human beings. As he wrote in his auto-biography: "I never doubted, for instance, the existence of the Deity, that he made the world and governed it by his Providence, that the most acceptable service of God was the doing of good to man, that our souls are immortal, and that *all crime will be punished and virtue rewarded either here or hereafter*" [emphasis added].

That is as succinct a statement of ethical monotheism as has ever been penned. Indeed, Franklin and many of America's founders were ethical monotheists. Their flaws notwith-standing, they were the type of people the Torah wants all people to be.

3. Do you believe in the God Who gave the Ten Commandments?

This question needs to be asked even though it is included in the first question—because if God never revealed His moral will, how would we know what behaviors He demands from us and what behaviors He judges as wrong?

None of these comments are judgments of individuals; they are judgments of the statement "I believe in God." There are people who do not believe in the God of the Torah, and, for that matter, people who believe in no God, who are fine individuals—just as there are people who believe in the God of the Torah who are not fine individuals. But the best moral hope for mankind is to bring as many people as possible to belief in the God introduced by the Torah and His moral teachings, beginning with the Ten Commandments. That is the mission of the Jewish people. But few Jews believe in that mission. With a few exceptions, the Jews are messengers who have forgotten their message. In their defense, most were never taught it.

> *With a few exceptions, the Jews are messengers who have forgotten their message. In their defense, most were never taught it.*

Do you believe the Jews have a mission to humanity?

If so, how would you define that mission?

If your response is "social justice" or *tikkun olam* ("repair of the world"), is there a distinctive Jewish way of achieving that goal? And does that differ from the mission of bringing the world to the Ten Commandments?

בְּיָד חֲזָקָה. זוֹ הַדֶּבֶר, כְּמָה שֶׁנֶּאֱמַר: הִנֵּה יַד־ה' הוֹיָה בְּמִקְנְךָ אֲשֶׁר בַּשָּׂדֶה, בַּסּוּסִים, בַּחֲמֹרִים, בַּגְּמַלִּים, בַּבָּקָר וּבַצֹּאן, דֶּבֶר כָּבֵד מְאֹד.

"With a strong hand"—this [refers to] the [plague of] pestilence, as it is stated (Exodus 9:3): "Behold the hand of the Lord is upon your herds that are in the field, upon the horses, upon the donkeys, upon the camels, upon the cattle and upon the flocks, [there will be] a very heavy pestilence."

וּבִזְרֹעַ נְטוּיָה. זוֹ הַחֶרֶב, כְּמָה שֶׁנֶּאֱמַר: וְחַרְבּוֹ שְׁלוּפָה בְּיָדוֹ, נְטוּיָה עַל־יְרוּשָׁלָיִם.

"And with an outstretched forearm" [refers to] the sword, as it is stated (I Chronicles 21:16): "And his sword was drawn in his hand, leaning over Jerusalem."

וּבְמוֹרָא גָּדֹל. זוֹ גִּלּוּי שְׁכִינָה. כְּמָה שֶׁנֶּאֱמַר, אוֹ הֲנִסָּה אֱלֹהִים לָבוֹא לָקַחַת לוֹ גוֹי מִקֶּרֶב גּוֹי בְּמַסֹּת בְּאֹתֹת וּבְמוֹפְתִים וּבְמִלְחָמָה וּבְיָד חֲזָקָה וּבִזְרוֹעַ נְטוּיָה וּבְמוֹרָאִים גְּדֹלִים כְּכֹל אֲשֶׁר־עָשָׂה לָכֶם ה' אֱלֹהֵיכֶם בְּמִצְרַיִם לְעֵינֶיךָ.

"And with great awe"—this [refers to the revelation of] the Divine Presence, as it is stated (Deuteronomy 4:34): "Or did God try to take for Himself a nation from within a nation with enigmas, with signs and with wonders and with war and with a strong hand and with an outstretched forearm and with great and awesome acts, like all that the Lord, your God, did for you in Egypt in front of your eyes?"

וּבְאֹתוֹת. זֶה הַמַּטֶּה, כְּמָה שֶׁנֶּאֱמַר: וְאֶת הַמַּטֶּה הַזֶּה תִּקַּח בְּיָדֶךָ, אֲשֶׁר תַּעֲשֶׂה־בּוֹ אֶת הָאֹתוֹת.

"And with signs"—this [refers to] the staff, as it is stated (Exodus 4:17): "And this staff you shall take in your hand, that with it you will perform signs."

וּבְמֹפְתִים. זֶה הַדָּם, כְּמָה שֶׁנֶּאֱמַר: וְנָתַתִּי מוֹפְתִים בַּשָּׁמַיִם וּבָאָרֶץ.

"And with wonders"—this [refers to] the blood, as it is stated (Joel 3:3): "And I will place my wonders in the heavens and on the earth."

The Ten Plagues

When you say the following words—"blood and fire and pillars of smoke"—and recite each of the ten plagues and their acronyms, remove some wine from your cup. This is traditionally done by inserting the little finger into the cup of wine when saying the words and then allowing a drop of wine to fall from the finger onto a plate. This is done to symbolically deprive ourselves of joy while recounting the suffering of the Egyptians. This humanizing of the Egyptians comes directly from the Torah, which commands Jews not to hate Egyptians (Deuteronomy 23:8).

דָּם וָאֵשׁ וְתִימְרוֹת עָשָׁן.

Blood and fire and pillars of smoke.

There were three major purposes for the ten plagues. The first and most obvious was to force Pharaoh and the Egyptians to release the Hebrews. The second was to punish Pharaoh and the Egyptians for the terrible suffering they had inflicted on the Israelites over hundreds of years—including, for a time, the murder of newborn Hebrew boys. God and the Torah believe in punishment when appropriate, because God and the Torah are preoccupied with justice. While the world needs compassion and other good traits, they must all be rooted in justice or we will end up with neither justice nor compassion. The third purpose of the plagues was to demonstrate to the Israelites (and to the Egyptians) that God, not the gods of Egypt (including Pharaoh), is the real God. That is why, as we have seen, the plagues were specifically directed against Egypt's gods.

דָּבָר אַחֵר: בְּיָד חֲזָקָה שְׁתַּיִם, וּבִזְרֹעַ נְטוּיָה שְׁתַּיִם, וּבְמֹרָא גָּדֹל – שְׁתַּיִם, וּבְאֹתוֹת – שְׁתַּיִם, וּבְמֹפְתִים – שְׁתַּיִם.

Another [explanation]: "With a strong hand" [corresponds to] two [plagues]; "and with an outstretched forearm" [corresponds to] two [plagues]; "and with great awe" [corresponds to] two [plagues]; "and with signs" [corresponds to] two [plagues]; "and with wonders" [corresponds to] two [plagues].

אֵלּוּ עֶשֶׂר מַכּוֹת שֶׁהֵבִיא הַקָּדוֹשׁ בָּרוּךְ הוּא עַל־הַמִּצְרִים בְּמִצְרַיִם, וְאֵלּוּ הֵן:

These are [the] ten plagues that the Holy One, blessed be He, brought on the Egyptians in Egypt and they are:

Blood	דָּם
Frogs	צְפַרְדֵּעַ
Lice	כִּנִּים
Flies/Insects	עָרוֹב
Pestilence	דֶּבֶר
Boils	שְׁחִין
Hail	בָּרָד
Locusts	אַרְבֶּה
Darkness	חֹשֶׁךְ
Slaying of the Firstborn	מַכַּת בְּכוֹרוֹת

רַבִּי יְהוּדָה הָיָה נוֹתֵן בָּהֶם סִמָּנִים: דְּצַ"ךְ עַד"שׁ בְּאַח"ב.

Rabbi Yehuda was accustomed to giving [the plagues] mnemonics: Detzakh [the Hebrew initials of the first three plagues], Adash [the Hebrew initials of the second three plagues], Be'a'chav [the Hebrew initials of the last four plagues].

The next three paragraphs describe three Talmudic rabbis' takes on how many plagues, in addition to the ten enumerated in the Torah, they believed God really brought down upon the Egyptians. (There is rarely much said about these three paragraphs at the Seder. Those not committed to reciting every word of the Haggadah may wish to proceed directly to the Dayenu song.)

רַבִּי יוֹסֵי הַגְּלִילִי אוֹמֵר: מִנַּיִן אַתָּה אוֹמֵר שֶׁלָּקוּ הַמִּצְרִים בְּמִצְרַיִם עֶשֶׂר מַכּוֹת וְעַל הַיָּם לָקוּ חֲמִשִּׁים מַכּוֹת? בְּמִצְרַיִם מַה הוּא אוֹמֵר? וַיֹּאמְרוּ הַחַרְטֻמִּם אֶל פַּרְעֹה: אֶצְבַּע אֱלֹהִים הוּא, וְעַל הַיָּם מָה הוּא אוֹמֵר? וַיַּרְא יִשְׂרָאֵל אֶת־הַיָּד הַגְּדֹלָה אֲשֶׁר עָשָׂה ה' בְּמִצְרַיִם, וַיִּירְאוּ הָעָם אֶת־ה', וַיַּאֲמִינוּ בַּיי וּבְמֹשֶׁה עַבְדּוֹ. כַּמָּה לָקוּ בָאֶצְבַּע? עֶשֶׂר מַכּוֹת. אֱמוֹר מֵעַתָּה: בְּמִצְרַיִם לָקוּ עֶשֶׂר מַכּוֹת וְעַל הַיָּם לָקוּ חֲמִשִּׁים מַכּוֹת.

Rabbi Yose HaGelili says, "From where can you [derive] that the Egyptians were struck with ten plagues in Egypt and struck with fifty plagues at the Sea? In Egypt, what does it state? 'Then the magicians said unto Pharaoh: "This is the finger of God"' (Exodus 8:15). And at the Sea, what does it state? 'And Israel saw the Lord's great hand that he used upon the Egyptians, and the people feared the Lord; and they believed in the Lord, and in Moses, His servant' (Exodus 14:31). How many were they struck with the finger? Ten plagues. You can say from here that in Egypt, they were struck with ten plagues and at the Sea, they were struck with fifty plagues."

רַבִּי אֱלִיעֶזֶר אוֹמֵר: מִנַּיִן שֶׁכָּל־מַכָּה וּמַכָּה שֶׁהֵבִיא הַקָּדוֹשׁ בָּרוּךְ הוּא עַל הַמִּצְרִים בְּמִצְרַיִם הָיְתָה שֶׁל אַרְבַּע מַכּוֹת? שֶׁנֶּאֱמַר: יְשַׁלַּח־בָּם חֲרוֹן אַפּוֹ, עֶבְרָה וָזַעַם וְצָרָה, מִשְׁלַחַת מַלְאֲכֵי רָעִים. עֶבְרָה – אַחַת, וָזַעַם – שְׁתַּיִם, וְצָרָה – שָׁלֹשׁ, מִשְׁלַחַת מַלְאֲכֵי רָעִים – אַרְבַּע. אֱמוֹר מֵעַתָּה: בְּמִצְרַיִם לָקוּ אַרְבָּעִים מַכּוֹת וְעַל הַיָּם לָקוּ מָאתַיִם מַכּוֹת.

Rabbi Eliezer says, "From where [can you derive] that every plague that the Holy One, blessed be He, brought upon the Egyptians in Egypt was [composed] of four plagues? As it is stated (Psalms 78:49): 'He sent upon them the fierceness of His anger, wrath, and fury, and trouble, a sending of messengers of evil.' 'Wrath' [corresponds to] one; 'and fury' is two; 'and trouble' is three; 'a sending of messengers of evil' is four. You can say from here that in Egypt, they were struck with forty plagues, and at the Sea, they were struck with two hundred plagues."

רַבִּי עֲקִיבָא אוֹמֵר: מִנַּיִן שֶׁכָּל־מַכָּה וּמַכָּה שֶׁהֵבִיא הַקָּדוֹשׁ בָּרוּךְ הוּא עַל הַמִּצְרִים בְּמִצְרַיִם הָיְתָה שֶׁל חָמֵשׁ מַכּוֹת? שֶׁנֶּאֱמַר: יְשַׁלַּח־בָּם חֲרוֹן אַפּוֹ, עֶבְרָה וָזַעַם וְצָרָה, מִשְׁלַחַת מַלְאֲכֵי רָעִים. חֲרוֹן אַפּוֹ – אַחַת, עֶבְרָה – שְׁתַּיִם, וָזַעַם – שָׁלֹשׁ, וְצָרָה – אַרְבַּע, מִשְׁלַחַת מַלְאֲכֵי רָעִים – חָמֵשׁ. אֱמוֹר מֵעַתָּה: בְּמִצְרַיִם לָקוּ חֲמִשִּׁים מַכּוֹת וְעַל הַיָּם לָקוּ חֲמִשִּׁים וּמָאתַיִם מַכּוֹת.

Rabbi Akiva says, "From where [can you derive] that every plague that the Holy One, blessed be He, brought upon the Egyptians in Egypt was [composed] of five plagues? As it is stated (Psalms 78:49): 'He sent upon them the fierceness of His anger, wrath, and fury, and trouble, a sending of messengers of evil.' 'The fierceness of His anger' [corresponds to] one; 'wrath' [brings it to] two; 'and fury' [brings it to] three; 'and trouble' [brings it to] four; 'a sending of messengers of evil' [brings it to] five. You can say from here that in Egypt, they were struck with fifty plagues and at the Sea, they were struck with two hundred and fifty plagues."

DAYENU
The Song of Gratitude

Dayenu is the best-known song of Passover. It is a list of fourteen wonderful things God did for the Jews during and after the Exodus. Each one ends with the Hebrew word *dayenu*, meaning, "It would be enough for us." (Note once again the use of the word "us," not "them.") It is difficult for anyone who does not speak Hebrew to imagine that one word can mean so many words in another language, but such is the case.

For Discussion
Gratitude—the Mother of Both Goodness and Happiness

If you think of all the people you know, you will not be able to name one who is ungrateful and happy.

People have been searching for the "secret to happiness" for much of recorded history. The secret is gratitude.

The purpose of this list is to inculcate gratitude in those who recite it. That the best-known song of Passover is solely about gratitude is instructive. The Rabbis understood the unique importance of gratitude. Everyone should. Gratitude is so important, it is the mother of two of the most important things in life: goodness and happiness. Only grateful people can be good, and only grateful people can be happy. Conversely, ungrateful people can be neither good nor happy. There is no such thing as a kind or happy ingrate.

We think that being unhappy leads people to complain, but it is truer to say that complaining leads people to become unhappy. The less gratitude one has, the more one sees oneself as a victim, and nothing is more likely to produce a bad and angry person or a bad and angry group than defining oneself or one's group as a victim. Victims too often believe they have a license to hurt others. As for happiness, if you think of all the people you know, you will not be able to name one who is ungrateful and happy. The two are mutually exclusive.

If gratitude is so important, how do we inculcate it in ourselves? One way is to expect little. The more we expect to have—from good health to good children to free things—the less we will be grateful for any of those things. Gratitude is largely dependent upon receiving what we do not expect to receive. That is why parents who give their children so much that the children come to expect more are actually depriving them of the ability to be happy—because they have deprived them of the ability to be grateful.

Another way to develop gratitude is to constantly express it. That is why it is so important to teach children to always say "thank you"—not only because it is the decent thing to do but because saying the words often enough inculcates gratitude in the person saying them.

This is one of the reasons that religion, when done correctly, is important to happiness: it regularly evokes gratitude. People who give thanks to God before each meal, as faithful Jews and Christians do, inculcate gratitude in themselves on a daily basis. Can a non-religious family invoke gratitude at each meal? In theory, yes. The family members can bow their heads and thank the farmer who planted and harvested their food, the truckers who shipped it to their city or town market, and the local supermarket. But I have never heard of a family doing so.

> *Most people remember the bad done to them far longer than the good done to them.*

Judaism also has a blessing of gratitude—the Modeh Ani—to be recited upon awakening each day: "Thank You, living and enduring God, for You have graciously returned my soul within me. Great is Your faithfulness."

But gratitude is difficult to sustain. Most people are grateful when someone does something particularly kind for them. But the more time passes, the less gratitude most people will have. Most people remember the bad done to them far longer than the good done to them.

Now it is time for all assembled at the Seder to express gratitude for the many good things God did for the Jews upon their leaving Egypt. But, as noted above, the song never refers to the recipients of God's goodness as "them," but as "us."

It clearly contains some hyperbole. Taken literally, some of these lines make no sense. But it is a good lesson in gratitude. Be grateful for any act another has done for you, even if it doesn't lead to the end result for which you had hoped.

כַּמָּה מַעֲלוֹת טוֹבוֹת לַמָּקוֹם עָלֵינוּ!

How many degrees of good did God do for us!

אִלּוּ הוֹצִיאָנוּ מִמִּצְרַיִם וְלֹא עָשָׂה בָהֶם שְׁפָטִים, דַּיֵּנוּ.

Dayenu #1: If He had taken us out of Egypt and not made judgments on [punished] them [the Egyptians], dayenu, it would have been enough for us.

אִלּוּ עָשָׂה בָהֶם שְׁפָטִים, וְלֹא עָשָׂה בֵאלֹהֵיהֶם, דַּיֵּנוּ.

Dayenu #2: If He had made judgments on them [the Egyptians] and had not made [them] on their gods [see pages 62–63], dayenu, it would have been enough for us.

אִלּוּ עָשָׂה בֵאלֹהֵיהֶם, וְלֹא הָרַג אֶת־בְּכוֹרֵיהֶם, דַּיֵּנוּ.

Dayenu #3: If He had [punished] their gods and had not killed their firstborn, dayenu, it would have been enough for us.

אִלּוּ הָרַג אֶת־בְּכוֹרֵיהֶם וְלֹא נָתַן לָנוּ אֶת־מָמוֹנָם, דַּיֵּנוּ.

Dayenu #4: If He had killed their firstborn and had not given us their money, dayenu, it would have been enough for us.

אִלּוּ נָתַן לָנוּ אֶת־מָמוֹנָם וְלֹא קָרַע לָנוּ אֶת־הַיָּם, דַּיֵּנוּ.

Dayenu #5: If He had given us their money and had not split the sea for us, dayenu, it would have been enough for us.

At this point, the Dayenu list seems to enter the world of hyperbole. If God had done all the miraculous things listed thus far but not split the sea, the Jews would have either been massacred by Pharaoh's army at the seashore or been brought back to Egypt as slaves. So it is not literally accurate to say that God doing all those things but not splitting the sea "would have been enough for us."

There is no doubt the Rabbis who composed this list were aware of these exaggerations. What concerned them was not internal logic, but enumerating all the great things God had done. What concerned them was inculcating gratitude—and providing a good life lesson that my son, David Prager, came up with. If your spouse works hard to make a beautiful meal—perhaps this Seder, for example—don't simply thank her (or him) "for making a beautiful meal (or Seder)." List some of the things you know she did to make it beautiful. Just as Jewish law requires a person seeking forgiveness to state precisely what he did wrong, when expressing gratitude one should state precisely the good things for which he or she is grateful.

אִלּוּ קָרַע לָנוּ אֶת־הַיָּם וְלֹא הֶעֱבִירָנוּ בְּתוֹכוֹ בֶּחָרָבָה, דַּיֵּנוּ.

Dayenu #6: If He had split the sea for us and had not taken us through it on dry land, dayenu, it would have been enough for us.

> *Just as Jewish law requires a person seeking forgiveness to state precisely what he did wrong, when expressing gratitude one should state precisely the good things for which he or she is grateful.*

אִלּוּ הֶעֱבִירָנוּ בְּתוֹכוֹ בֶּחָרָבָה וְלֹא שִׁקַּע צָרֵנוּ בְּתוֹכוֹ דַּיֵּנוּ.

Dayenu #7: If He had taken us through it on dry land and had not pushed down our enemies in the sea, dayenu, it would have been enough for us.

אִלּוּ שִׁקַּע צָרֵנוּ בְּתוֹכוֹ וְלֹא סִפֵּק צָרְכֵּנוּ בַּמִּדְבָּר אַרְבָּעִים שָׁנָה דַּיֵּנוּ.

Dayenu #8: If He had pushed down our enemies in [the sea] and had not supplied our needs in the wilderness for forty years, dayenu, it would have been enough for us.

אִלּוּ סִפֵּק צָרְכֵּנוּ בְּמִדְבָּר אַרְבָּעִים שָׁנָה וְלֹא הֶאֱכִילָנוּ אֶת־הַמָּן דַּיֵּנוּ.

Dayenu #9: If He had supplied our needs in the wilderness for forty years and had not fed us the manna, dayenu, it would have been enough for us.

Again, this is not literally true. It would not "have been enough for us" if God had not fed us. Also, there is an internal contradiction here. Since food and water are people's two most basic needs, how could God supply "our needs" and not give the Israelites manna, the food that sustained them in the desert?

אִלּוּ הֶאֱכִילָנוּ אֶת־הַמָּן וְלֹא נָתַן לָנוּ אֶת־הַשַּׁבָּת, דַּיֵּנוּ.

Dayenu #10: If He had fed us the manna and had not given us Shabbat, dayenu, it would have been enough for us.

אִלּוּ נָתַן לָנוּ אֶת־הַשַּׁבָּת, וְלֹא קֵרְבָנוּ לִפְנֵי הַר סִינַי, דַּיֵּנוּ.

Dayenu #11: If He had given us Shabbat and had not brought us close to Mount Sinai, dayenu, it would have been enough for us.

אִלּוּ קֵרְבָנוּ לִפְנֵי הַר סִינַי, וְלֹא נָתַן לָנוּ אֶת־הַתּוֹרָה. דַּיֵּנוּ.

Dayenu #12: If He had brought us close to Mount Sinai and had not given us the Torah, dayenu, it would have been enough for us.

אִלּוּ נָתַן לָנוּ אֶת־הַתּוֹרָה וְלֹא הִכְנִיסָנוּ לְאֶרֶץ יִשְׂרָאֵל, דַּיֵּנוּ.

Dayenu #13: If He had given us the Torah and had not brought us into the land of Israel, dayenu, it would have been enough for us.

אִלּוּ הִכְנִיסָנוּ לְאֶרֶץ יִשְׂרָאֵל וְלֹא בָנָה לָנוּ אֶת־בֵּית הַבְּחִירָה דַּיֵּנוּ.

Dayenu #14: If He had brought us into the land of Israel and had not built us the "Chosen House" [the Temple], dayenu, it would have been enough for us.

עַל אַחַת, כַּמָּה וְכַמָּה, טוֹבָה כְפוּלָה וּמְכֻפֶּלֶת לַמָּקוֹם עָלֵינוּ: שֶׁהוֹצִיאָנוּ מִמִּצְרַיִם, וְעָשָׂה בָהֶם שְׁפָטִים, וְעָשָׂה בֵאלֹהֵיהֶם, וְהָרַג אֶת־בְּכוֹרֵיהֶם, וְנָתַן לָנוּ אֶת־מָמוֹנָם, וְקָרַע לָנוּ אֶת־הַיָּם, וְהֶעֱבִירָנוּ בְּתוֹכוֹ בֶּחָרָבָה, וְשִׁקַּע צָרֵנוּ בְּתוֹכוֹ, וְסִפֵּק צָרְכֵּנוּ בַּמִּדְבָּר אַרְבָּעִים שָׁנָה, וְהֶאֱכִילָנוּ אֶת־הַמָּן, וְנָתַן לָנוּ אֶת־הַשַּׁבָּת, וְקֵרְבָנוּ לִפְנֵי הַר סִינַי, וְנָתַן לָנוּ אֶת־הַתּוֹרָה, וְהִכְנִיסָנוּ לְאֶרֶץ יִשְׂרָאֵל, וּבָנָה לָנוּ אֶת־בֵּית הַבְּחִירָה לְכַפֵּר עַל־כָּל־עֲוֹנוֹתֵינוּ׃

How much more so is the good that is doubled and quadrupled that God bestowed upon us: That He took us out of Egypt, made judgments upon them, made judgments upon their gods, killed their firstborn, gave us their money, split the sea for us, brought us through it on dry land, pushed our enemies [into the sea], supplied our needs in the wilderness for forty years, fed us the manna, gave us Shabbat, brought us close to Mount Sinai, gave us the Torah, brought us into the land of Israel, and built us the "Chosen House" [the Temple] to atone for all of our sins.

The Passover Sacrifice, *Matzah*, and *Maror*

רַבָּן גַּמְלִיאֵל הָיָה אוֹמֵר: כָּל שֶׁלֹּא אָמַר שְׁלֹשָׁה דְבָרִים אֵלּוּ בַּפֶּסַח, לֹא יָצָא יְדֵי חוֹבָתוֹ, וְאֵלּוּ הֵן: פֶּסַח, מַצָּה, וּמָרוֹר.

Rabban Gamliel would say: "Anyone who has not said these three things on Pesach has not fulfilled his obligation: 'the Pesach sacrifice, matzah and maror.'"

Pesach (the Passover Sacrifice)

פֶּסַח שֶׁהָיוּ אֲבוֹתֵינוּ אוֹכְלִים בִּזְמַן שֶׁבֵּית הַמִּקְדָּשׁ הָיָה קַיָּם, עַל שׁוּם מָה? עַל שׁוּם שֶׁפָּסַח הַקָּדוֹשׁ בָּרוּךְ הוּא עַל בָּתֵּי אֲבוֹתֵינוּ בְּמִצְרַיִם, שֶׁנֶּאֱמַר: וַאֲמַרְתֶּם זֶבַח פֶּסַח הוּא לַה', אֲשֶׁר פָּסַח עַל בָּתֵּי בְנֵי יִשְׂרָאֵל בְּמִצְרַיִם בְּנָגְפּוֹ אֶת־מִצְרַיִם, וְאֶת־בָּתֵּינוּ הִצִּיל וַיִּקֹּד הָעָם וַיִּשְׁתַּחֲווּ.

The Pesach [Passover] sacrifice that our ancestors were accustomed to eating when the Temple existed, for the sake of what was it? For the sake [to commemorate] that the Holy One, blessed be He, passed over the homes of our ancestors in Egypt, as it is stated (Exodus 12:27): "And you shall say: 'It is the Passover sacrifice to the Lord, for that He passed over the homes of the Children of Israel in Egypt, when He smote the Egyptians, and our homes he saved. And the people lowered their heads and bowed down.'"

This sacrifice was of a sheep. As sheep were sacred Egyptian animals, the Egyptians would have been infuriated by the sacrifice of a ram (a ram is an adult male sheep, and a lamb is a baby sheep). For this reason, the Israelites were told to sacrifice lambs before the eyes of their Egyptian oppressors to show both Egyptians and Hebrews whose God was genuine.

The Israelites were instructed to acquire the lamb on the tenth day of the month, but they were not allowed to slaughter it until the evening of the fourteenth day, four days later. The lamb's blood was to be used for marking the doors of the Israelites, and the lamb itself was to be roasted for the evening meal. This waiting period might have been intended to test the Israelites' faith: Could they maintain a faith in God that was stronger than their fear of the Egyptians, who could attack them at any moment for preparing to slaughter one of their gods?

The waiting period between acquiring and slaughtering the lamb was also a lesson in delayed gratification. Given that slaves are underfed and given the cheapest food, any delay in slaughtering, roasting, and consuming a lamb required genuine self-discipline. This delayed gratification is emulated at the Passover Seder. One of the Seder's components is an elaborate meal, but it is not eaten until the first half of the Haggadah is recited—which, depending on how much of the Haggadah is recited and how much discussion ensues, can easily take two hours.

Matzah (the Unleavened Bread)

Hold the *matzah* and show it to the others.

מַצָּה זוֹ שֶׁאָנוּ אוֹכְלִים, עַל שׁוּם מַה? עַל שׁוּם שֶׁלֹּא הִסְפִּיק בְּצֵקָם שֶׁל אֲבוֹתֵינוּ לְהַחֲמִיץ עַד שֶׁנִּגְלָה עֲלֵיהֶם מֶלֶךְ מַלְכֵי הַמְּלָכִים, הַקָּדוֹשׁ בָּרוּךְ הוּא, וּגְאָלָם, שֶׁנֶּאֱמַר: וַיֹּאפוּ אֶת־הַבָּצֵק אֲשֶׁר הוֹצִיאוּ מִמִּצְרַיִם עֻגֹת מַצּוֹת, כִּי לֹא חָמֵץ, כִּי גֹרְשׁוּ מִמִּצְרַיִם וְלֹא יָכְלוּ לְהִתְמַהְמֵהַּ, וְגַם צֵדָה לֹא עָשׂוּ לָהֶם.

This matzah that we are eating, for the sake of what [is it]? For the sake [to commemorate] that our ancestors' dough was not yet able to rise, before the King of kings, the Holy One, blessed be He, revealed [Himself] to them and redeemed them, as it is stated (Exodus 12:39): "And they baked the dough which they brought out of Egypt into matzah *cakes, since it did not rise; because they were expelled from Egypt, and could not tarry, neither had they made for themselves provisions."*

Leavening, a process believed to have been invented in Egypt about five hundred years before the Exodus, involves the fermentation of dough. Fermentation is a form of decomposition, and therefore represents decay and death. Egypt was known for its obsession with death: the best-known symbols of ancient Egypt are the pyramids, which are tombs, and its holiest book was *The Book of the Dead*. The Torah, in contrast, is rooted in the affirmation of life.

The avoidance of leaven during Passover may be seen as a symbolic rejection of the Egyptian preoccupation with death. Much Torah law and teaching is a rejection of the values of Egypt, most particularly its emphasis on death and on the worship of nature. The Torah is preoccupied with separating that which represents death from that which represents life.

The Torah and later Judaism, therefore, enacted numerous ritual laws to separate the two.

Examples include the draining of the blood from an animal before it is eaten ("For the life of all flesh is its blood"—Leviticus 17:14 and Genesis 9:4); the prohibition on Jewish priests from coming into contact with the dead, as they are to be preoccupied only with life; and the separation of milk and meat (milk, which comes from a living creature and which gives life, represents life; meat, which comes from a carcass, represents death).

Maror (the Bitter Herbs)

Hold the *maror* and show it to the others.

מָרוֹר זֶה שֶׁאָנוּ אוֹכְלִים, עַל שׁוּם מַה? עַל שׁוּם שֶׁמֵּרְרוּ הַמִּצְרִים אֶת־חַיֵּי אֲבוֹתֵינוּ בְּמִצְרָיִם, שֶׁנֶּאֱמַר: וַיְמָרְרוּ אֶת חַיֵּיהֶם בַּעֲבֹדָה קָשָׁה, בְּחֹמֶר וּבִלְבֵנִים וּבְכָל־עֲבֹדָה בַּשָּׂדֶה אֵת כָּל־עֲבֹדָתָם אֲשֶׁר עָבְדוּ בָהֶם בְּפָרֶךְ.

This maror [bitter herbs] that we are eating—why? Because the Egyptians embittered the lives of our ancestors in Egypt, as it is stated (Exodus 1:14): "And they made their lives bitter with hard service, in mortar and in brick, and in all manner of service in the field; in all their service, wherein they made them serve with rigor."

Judaism is a physical religion because humans are physical beings. To symbolize what it was like to be a slave, taste bitter food. To know what the unleavened bread tasted like, eat *matzah*. On Passover, we are to experience in some way what the Israelites experienced in Egypt. On Sukkot, we are to eat (and some even sleep) in a *sukkah* (booth) to experience what our ancestors experienced traveling in the wilderness.

בְּכָל־דּוֹר וָדוֹר חַיָּב אָדָם לִרְאוֹת אֶת־עַצְמוֹ כְּאִלּוּ הוּא יָצָא מִמִּצְרַיִם.

In each and every generation, a person is obligated to see himself as if he left Egypt.

This is one of the best-known statements in the Haggadah—for good reason. In one sentence it encapsulates the key moment of Jewish history, as well as of the Seder. We are to see ourselves as having exited Egypt. Again, this didn't happen to *them*, but to *us*. Nothing has ensured Jewish continuity more than this way of looking at Jewish history.

This way of looking at history accomplishes something else of vital importance. When the Jew sees himself as having been taken out of Egypt, he becomes grateful to God. As noted above, gratitude is indispensable to a good life. But there is something else going on here. There have not been many exoduses since the Exodus. A Jew can all too easily abandon gratitude to God given the amount of Jewish suffering since then. By reliving the Exodus every year of their lives and in every generation, the Jews are more likely to remain grateful to a God Who seems too often to have since abandoned His people.

שֶׁנֶּאֱמַר: וְהִגַּדְתָּ לְבִנְךָ בַּיּוֹם הַהוּא לֵאמֹר, בַּעֲבוּר זֶה עָשָׂה ה' לִי בְּצֵאתִי מִמִּצְרָיִם. לֹא אֶת־אֲבוֹתֵינוּ בִּלְבָד גָּאַל הַקָּדוֹשׁ בָּרוּךְ הוּא, אֶלָּא אַף אוֹתָנוּ גָּאַל עִמָּהֶם, שֶׁנֶּאֱמַר: וְאוֹתָנוּ הוֹצִיא מִשָּׁם, לְמַעַן הָבִיא אוֹתָנוּ, לָתֶת לָנוּ אֶת־הָאָרֶץ אֲשֶׁר נִשְׁבַּע לַאֲבֹתֵינוּ.

As it says: "And you will tell your child on that day, 'For the sake of this, did the Lord do [this] for me in my going out of Egypt'" (Exodus 13:8). The Holy One, blessed be He, did not only liberate our ancestors but us with them. As it says: "And He took us out from there in order to bring us [and] give us the land He swore to our fathers" (Deuteronomy 6:23).

Hold the cup in your hand, cover the *matzah*, and say:

לְפִיכָךְ אֲנַחְנוּ חַיָּבִים לְהוֹדוֹת, לְהַלֵּל, לְשַׁבֵּחַ, לְפָאֵר, לְרוֹמֵם, לְהַדֵּר, לְבָרֵךְ, לְעַלֵּה וּלְקַלֵּס לְמִי שֶׁעָשָׂה לַאֲבוֹתֵינוּ וְלָנוּ אֶת־כָּל־הַנִּסִּים הָאֵלּוּ: הוֹצִיאָנוּ מֵעַבְדוּת לְחֵרוּת מִיָּגוֹן לְשִׂמְחָה, וּמֵאֵבֶל לְיוֹם טוֹב, וּמֵאֲפֵלָה לְאוֹר גָּדוֹל, וּמִשִּׁעְבּוּד לִגְאֻלָּה. וְנֹאמַר לְפָנָיו שִׁירָה חֲדָשָׁה: הַלְלוּיָהּ.

Therefore, we are obligated to thank, praise, laud, glorify, exalt, lavish, bless, raise high, and acclaim He who made all these miracles for our ancestors and for us: He brought us out from slavery to freedom, from sorrow to joy, from mourning to [celebration of] a festival, from darkness to great light, and from servitude to redemption. And let us say a new song before Him, Halleluyah!

Hallel (Psalms Part I)

הַלְלוּיָהּ הַלְלוּ עַבְדֵי ה', הַלְלוּ אֶת־שֵׁם ה'. יְהִי שֵׁם ה' מְבֹרָךְ מֵעַתָּה וְעַד עוֹלָם. מִמִּזְרַח שֶׁמֶשׁ עַד מְבוֹאוֹ מְהֻלָּל שֵׁם ה'. רָם עַל־כָּל־גּוֹיִם ה', עַל הַשָּׁמַיִם כְּבוֹדוֹ. מִי כַּיי אֱלֹהֵינוּ הַמַּגְבִּיהִי לָשָׁבֶת, הַמַּשְׁפִּילִי לִרְאוֹת בַּשָּׁמַיִם וּבָאָרֶץ? מְקִימִי מֵעָפָר דָּל, מֵאַשְׁפֹּת יָרִים אֶבְיוֹן, לְהוֹשִׁיבִי עִם־נְדִיבִים, עִם נְדִיבֵי עַמּוֹ. מוֹשִׁיבִי עֲקֶרֶת הַבַּיִת, אֵם הַבָּנִים שְׂמֵחָה. הַלְלוּיָהּ.

Halleluyah! Praise, servants of the Lord, praise the name of the Lord. May the Name of the Lord be blessed from now and forever. From the rising of the sun in the East to its setting, the name of the Lord is praised. Above all nations is the Lord, His honor is above the heavens. Who is like the Lord, our God, Who sits on high; Who looks down upon the heavens and the earth? He brings up the poor out of the dirt; from the refuse piles, He raises the destitute. To seat him with the nobles, with the nobles of his people. He seats a barren woman in a home, a happy mother of children. Halleluyah! (Psalm 113)

בְּצֵאת יִשְׂרָאֵל מִמִּצְרָיִם, בֵּית יַעֲקֹב מֵעַם לֹעֵז, הָיְתָה יְהוּדָה לְקָדְשׁוֹ, יִשְׂרָאֵל מַמְשְׁלוֹתָיו. הַיָּם רָאָה וַיָּנֹס, הַיַּרְדֵּן יִסֹּב לְאָחוֹר. הֶהָרִים רָקְדוּ כְאֵילִים, גְּבָעוֹת כִּבְנֵי צֹאן. מַה לְּךָ הַיָּם כִּי תָנוּס, הַיַּרְדֵּן – תִּסֹּב לְאָחוֹר, הֶהָרִים – תִּרְקְדוּ כְאֵילִים, גְּבָעוֹת כִּבְנֵי־צֹאן. מִלִּפְנֵי אָדוֹן חוּלִי אָרֶץ, מִלִּפְנֵי אֱלוֹהַּ יַעֲקֹב. הַהֹפְכִי הַצּוּר אֲגַם־מָיִם, חַלָּמִישׁ לְמַעְיְנוֹ־מָיִם.

In Israel's going out from Egypt, the house of Jacob from a people of foreign speech. Judah became His holy one, Israel, His dominion. The sea saw and fled, the Jordan turned to the rear. The mountains danced like rams, the hills like young sheep. What is happening to you, O sea, that you are fleeing, O Jordan that you turn to the rear; O mountains that you dance like rams, O hills like young sheep? From before the Master, tremble O earth, from before the Lord of Jacob. He who turns the boulder into a pond of water, the flint into a spring of water. (Psalm 114)

The Second Cup of Wine

Recite the following two blessings holding the cup of wine.

בָּרוּךְ אַתָּה ה' אֱלֹהֵינוּ מֶלֶךְ הָעוֹלָם, אֲשֶׁר גְּאָלָנוּ וְגָאַל אֶת־אֲבוֹתֵינוּ מִמִּצְרַיִם,
וְהִגִּיעָנוּ הַלַּיְלָה הַזֶּה לֶאֱכָל־בּוֹ מַצָּה וּמָרוֹר. כֵּן ה' אֱלֹהֵינוּ וֵאלֹהֵי אֲבוֹתֵינוּ
יַגִּיעֵנוּ לְמוֹעֲדִים וְלִרְגָלִים אֲחֵרִים הַבָּאִים לִקְרָאתֵנוּ לְשָׁלוֹם, שְׂמֵחִים בְּבִנְיַן עִירֶךְ
וְשָׂשִׂים בַּעֲבוֹדָתֶךָ. וְנֹאכַל שָׁם מִן הַזְּבָחִים וּמִן הַפְּסָחִים אֲשֶׁר יַגִּיעַ דָּמָם עַל קִיר
מִזְבַּחֲךָ לְרָצוֹן, וְנוֹדֶה לְךָ שִׁיר חָדָשׁ עַל גְּאֻלָּתֵנוּ וְעַל פְּדוּת נַפְשֵׁנוּ. בָּרוּךְ אַתָּה
ה', גָּאַל יִשְׂרָאֵל.

*Blessed are You, Lord our God, King of the universe, Who redeemed us and redeemed
our ancestors from Egypt, and brought us on this night to eat* matzah *and* maror; *so
too, Lord our God, and God of our ancestors, bring us to other appointed times and
holidays that will come to greet us in peace, joyful in the building of Your city and
happy in Your worship; that we shall eat there from the offerings and from the Pesach
sacrifices, the blood of which shall reach the wall of Your altar for favor, and we shall
thank You with a new song upon our redemption and upon the restoration of our
souls. Blessed are You, Lord, Who redeemed Israel.*

בָּרוּךְ אַתָּה ה', אֱלֹהֵינוּ מֶלֶךְ הָעוֹלָם בּוֹרֵא פְּרִי הַגָּפֶן.

Blessed are You, Lord our God, Who creates the fruit of the vine.

(Baruch ata Adonai, Eloheinu melech ha'olam bo'rei pri ha'gafen.)

רחצה

RACHTZAH
Washing

Unlike the earlier washing, this is the traditional washing of the hands prior to eating, and there-fore includes the traditional blessing over washing. Pour water three times over each hand, begin-ning with the right hand, and recite this blessing:

בָּרוּךְ אַתָּה ה', אֱלֹהֵינוּ מֶלֶךְ הָעוֹלָם, אֲשֶׁר קִדְּשָׁנוּ בְּמִצְוֹתָיו וְצִוָּנוּ עַל
נְטִילַת יָדָיִם.

Blessed are You, Lord our God, King of the Universe, Who has sanctified us with His commandments and has commanded us about washing our hands.

(Baruch ata Adonai, Eloheinu melech ha'olam, asher kidishanu bimitzvotav vitzivanu all nitilat yadayim.)

מוציא מצה
MOTZI MATZAH
Taking Out the *Matzah*

Take out the three *matzahs*, the broken one between the two whole ones. Holding the three of them, recite the following blessing and then eat from the top *matzah*.

בָּרוּךְ אַתָּה ה', אֱלֹהֵינוּ מֶלֶךְ הָעוֹלָם הַמּוֹצִיא לֶחֶם מִן הָאָרֶץ.

Blessed are You, Lord our God, King of the Universe, Who brings forth bread from the ground.

(Baruch ata Adonai, Eloheinu melech ha'olam ha'motzee lechem min ha'aretz.)

Recite the following blessing and then eat from the broken *matzah*.

בָּרוּךְ אַתָּה ה', אֱלֹהֵינוּ מֶלֶךְ הָעוֹלָם, אֲשֶׁר קִדְּשָׁנוּ בְּמִצְוֹתָיו וְצִוָּנוּ עַל אֲכִילַת מַצָּה.

Blessed are You, Lord our God, King of the Universe, Who has sanctified us with His commandments and has commanded us on the eating of matzah.

(Baruch ata Adonai, Eloheinu melech ha'olam asher kidishanu b'mitz'votav v'tzivanu al achilat matzah.)

מרור
MAROR
Bitter Herbs

All present should take a *ke'zayit* (olive-sized piece) of *maror*, dip it into the *haroset*, make the blessing, and eat.

בָּרוּךְ אַתָּה ה', אֱלֹהֵינוּ מֶלֶךְ הָעוֹלָם, אֲשֶׁר קִדְּשָׁנוּ בְּמִצְוֹתָיו וְצִוָּנוּ עַל אֲכִילַת מָרוֹר.

Blessed are You, Lord our God, King of the Universe, Who has sanctified us with His commandments and commanded us about eating maror.

(Baruch ata Adonai, Eloheinu melech ha'olam asher kidishanu b'mitz'votav v'tzivanu al achilat maror.)

כּוֹרֵךְ
KORECH
Sandwich

All present take a *ke'zayit* (olive-sized piece) from the third whole *matzah* with a *ke'zayit* of *maror*, combine them, and, before eating, recite:

זֵכֶר לְמִקְדָּשׁ כְּהִלֵּל. כֵּן עָשָׂה הִלֵּל בִּזְמַן שֶׁבֵּית הַמִּקְדָּשׁ הָיָה קַיָּם.

In memory of the Temple according to Hillel. This is what Hillel would do when the Temple existed:

הָיָה כּוֹרֵךְ (פֶּסַח) מַצָּה וּמָרוֹר וְאוֹכֵל בְּיַחַד, לְקַיֵּם מַה שֶּׁנֶּאֱמַר: עַל מַצּוֹת וּמְרוֹרִים יֹאכְלֻהוּ.

He would combine the (Passover offering with) matzah and maror and eat them together, in order to fulfill what is stated in Numbers 9:11, "You should eat it upon matzot and marorim," and in Exodus 12:8, "They shall eat the flesh that same night; they shall eat it roasted over the fire, with unleavened bread and with bitter herbs."

שלחן עורך
SHULCHAN ORECH (THE SET TABLE)
The Seder Meal

Now is the time everyone has been waiting for—the great Passover Seder meal. The amount of work put into preparing the Seder meal is prodigious, work that has traditionally been done by the woman of the house. This led my mother, Hilda Prager, of blessed memory, to once quip: "Only the men got out of Egypt."

During the meal, participants are welcome to discuss anything they wish. People may want to continue some of the discussions prompted by ideas addressed above, reminisce about past Seders, or catch up with what is new in the lives of fellow guests not seen since last Passover or, for that matter, ever, in the case of new participants.

צפון
TZAFUN
The Concealed (*Matzah*)

When the Seder meal ends, everyone eats a piece of the *afikoman*, the *matzah* concealed at the beginning of the Seder. When children are present, usually one or more of them will have "stolen" the *afikoman*, and since the Seder cannot continue without the *afikoman*, the children ask for something in exchange for returning it.

Before eating the *afikoman*, the following is said:

זֵכֶר לְקָרְבָּן פֶּסַח הַנֶּאֱכָל עַל הַשּׂוֹבַע.

In memory of the Pesach sacrifice that was eaten upon being satiated.

ברך
BARECH (BLESSING OVER THE FOOD)
ברכת המזון
Birkat HaMazon

Pour the third cup of wine and recite the Grace over the Food.

שִׁיר הַמַּעֲלוֹת, בְּשׁוּב ה' אֶת שִׁיבַת צִיּוֹן הָיִינוּ כְּחֹלְמִים. אָז יִמָּלֵא שְׂחוֹק פִּינוּ
וּלְשׁוֹנֵנוּ רִנָּה. אָז יֹאמְרוּ בַגּוֹיִם: הִגְדִּיל ה' לַעֲשׂוֹת עִם אֵלֶּה. הִגְדִּיל ה' לַעֲשׂוֹת
עִמָּנוּ, הָיִינוּ שְׂמֵחִים. שׁוּבָה ה' אֶת שְׁבִיתֵנוּ כַּאֲפִיקִים בַּנֶּגֶב. הַזֹּרְעִים בְּדִמְעָה,
בְּרִנָּה יִקְצֹרוּ. הָלוֹךְ יֵלֵךְ וּבָכֹה נֹשֵׂא מֶשֶׁךְ הַזָּרַע, בֹּא יָבֹא בְרִנָּה נֹשֵׂא אֲלֻמֹּתָיו.

A Song of Ascents; When the Lord will bring back the captivity of Zion, we will be like dreamers. Then our mouth will be full of mirth and our tongue [a] joyful melody; then they will say among the nations, "The Lord has done greatly with these." The Lord has done great things with us; we are happy. Lord, return our captivity like streams in the desert. Those that sow with tears will reap with joyful song. He who surely goes and cries, he carries the measure of seed, he will surely come in joyful song and carry his sheaves (Psalm 126).

If three or more over the age of bar-mitzvah partook of the meal, one of them (the "leader") opens the Birkat HaMazon by saying:

רַבּוֹתַי נְבָרֵךְ.

Fellow teachers, let us bless:

Those present respond:

יְהִי שֵׁם ה' מְבֹרָךְ מֵעַתָּה וְעַד עוֹלָם.

May the Name of the Lord be blessed from now and forever. (Psalm 113:2)

Y'hi shem Adonai m'vorach mei-atah v'ad olam.

The leader:

יְהִי שֵׁם ה' מְבֹרָךְ מֵעַתָּה וְעַד עוֹלָם.
בִּרְשׁוּת מָרָנָן וְרַבָּנָן וְרַבּוֹתַי, נְבָרֵךְ [אֱלֹהֵינוּ] שֶׁאָכַלְנוּ מִשֶּׁלּוֹ.

May the Name of the Lord be blessed from now and forever.

With the permission of our gentlemen, our teachers, and my teachers, let us bless [our God] from Whom we have eaten.

Those present respond:

בָּרוּךְ [אֱלֹהֵינוּ] שֶׁאָכַלְנוּ מִשֶּׁלּוֹ וּבְטוּבוֹ חָיִינוּ.

Blessed is [our God] from Whom we have eaten and from Whose goodness we live.

Baruch [Eloheinu] she-achalnu mishelo uv'tuvo chayinu.

The leader:

בָּרוּךְ [אֱלֹהֵינוּ] שֶׁאָכַלְנוּ מִשֶּׁלּוֹ וּבְטוּבוֹ חָיִינוּ.

Blessed is [our God] from Whom we have eaten and from Whose goodness we live.

The leader:

בָּרוּךְ הוּא וּבָרוּךְ שְׁמוֹ.

Blessed is He and blessed is His name.

Participants recite to themselves or sing together the Birkat HaMazon until page 102.

בָּרוּךְ אַתָּה ה', אֱלֹהֵינוּ מֶלֶךְ הָעוֹלָם, הַזָּן אֶת הָעוֹלָם כֻּלּוֹ בְּטוּבוֹ בְּחֵן בְּחֶסֶד
וּבְרַחֲמִים, הוּא נוֹתֵן לֶחֶם לְכָל בָּשָׂר כִּי לְעוֹלָם חַסְדּוֹ. וּבְטוּבוֹ הַגָּדוֹל תָּמִיד לֹא

חָסַר לָנוּ, וְאַל יֶחְסַר לָנוּ מָזוֹן לְעוֹלָם וָעֶד. בַּעֲבוּר שְׁמוֹ הַגָּדוֹל, כִּי הוּא אֵל זָן וּמְפַרְנֵס לַכֹּל וּמֵטִיב לַכֹּל, וּמֵכִין מָזוֹן לְכָל בְּרִיּוֹתָיו אֲשֶׁר בָּרָא. בָּרוּךְ אַתָּה ה', הַזָּן אֶת הַכֹּל.

Blessed are You, Lord our God, King of the Universe, Who nourishes the entire world in His goodness, in grace, in kindness and in mercy; He gives bread to all flesh since His kindness is forever. And in His great goodness, we always have not lacked, and may we not lack nourishment forever and always, because of His great name. Since He is a Power that feeds and provides for all and does good to all and prepares nourishment for all of his creatures that he created. Blessed are You, Lord, Who sustains all.

נוֹדֶה לְךָ ה' אֱלֹהֵינוּ עַל שֶׁהִנְחַלְתָּ לַאֲבוֹתֵינוּ אֶרֶץ חֶמְדָּה טוֹבָה וּרְחָבָה, וְעַל שֶׁהוֹצֵאתָנוּ ה' אֱלֹהֵינוּ מֵאֶרֶץ מִצְרַיִם, וּפְדִיתָנוּ מִבֵּית עֲבָדִים, וְעַל בְּרִיתְךָ שֶׁחָתַמְתָּ בִּבְשָׂרֵנוּ, וְעַל תּוֹרָתְךָ שֶׁלִּמַּדְתָּנוּ, וְעַל חֻקֶּיךָ שֶׁהוֹדַעְתָּנוּ, וְעַל חַיִּים חֵן וָחֶסֶד שֶׁחוֹנַנְתָּנוּ, וְעַל אֲכִילַת מָזוֹן שָׁאַתָּה זָן וּמְפַרְנֵס אוֹתָנוּ תָּמִיד, בְּכָל יוֹם וּבְכָל עֵת וּבְכָל שָׁעָה.

We thank you, Lord our God, that You have given as an inheritance to our ancestors a lovely, good, and broad land, and that You took us out, Lord our God, from the land of Egypt, and that You redeemed us from a house of slaves, and for Your covenant which You have sealed in our flesh, and for Your Torah that You have taught us, and for Your statutes which You have made known to us, and for life, grace, and kindness that You have granted us, and for the eating of nourishment that You feed and provide for us always, on all days, and at all times and in every hour.

וְעַל הַכֹּל ה' אֱלֹהֵינוּ, אֲנַחְנוּ מוֹדִים לָךְ וּמְבָרְכִים אוֹתָךְ, יִתְבָּרַךְ שִׁמְךָ בְּפִי כָּל חַי תָּמִיד לְעוֹלָם וָעֶד.

And for everything, Lord our God, we thank You and bless You; may Your name be blessed by the mouth of all life, constantly forever.

For Discussion
God and Judaism Want Us to Enjoy Life

כְּכָּתוּב: וְאָכַלְתָּ וְשָׂבָעְתָּ וּבֵרַכְתָּ אֶת ה' אֱלֹהֶיךָ עַל הָאָרֶץ הַטּוֹבָה אֲשֶׁר נָתַן לָךְ.

As it is written (Deuteronomy 8:10): "And you shall eat and be satisfied and bless the Lord your God for the good land He has given you."

Note that the Torah verse cited in this paragraph of the Birkat HaMazon says, "You shall eat and be satisfied and bless the Lord. . . ." Why are the words "and be satisfied" included? Wouldn't the verse make perfect sense if it simply stated, "You shall eat and bless the Lord . . ."?

The answer is that God and the Torah want us to enjoy life. We are not just to eat enough to sustain our lives. We should enjoy eating—because God wants us to enjoy life. Judaism teaches that we should enjoy every permitted pleasure. According to the Talmud, when we are judged in the afterlife, we will be asked why we did not partake of every permitted pleasure.[16]

Unfortunately, many religious people—of all faiths—equate denial of pleasure (asceticism) with piety. These people give religion a bad name. If the purpose of any given religion is to deny oneself as much joy as possible, why would emotionally healthy people want to be a member of that religion? The answer is that they wouldn't. In fact, unhappy religious people are one of the best arguments for not living a religious life. Conversely, happy religious people are among the best arguments for living a religious life.

The Torah repeatedly commands—yes, commands—the Jew to be happy. In keeping with that spirit, later Judaism instructs the Jew to do something quite remarkable: delay the week of mourning (*shiva*) after the death of an immediate relative during Shabbat.

בָּרוּךְ אַתָּה ה', עַל הָאָרֶץ וְעַל הַמָּזוֹן.

Blessed are You, Lord, for the land and for the nourishment.

רַחֵם נָא ה' אֱלֹהֵינוּ עַל יִשְׂרָאֵל עַמֶּךָ וְעַל יְרוּשָׁלַיִם עִירֶךָ וְעַל צִיּוֹן מִשְׁכַּן כְּבוֹדֶךָ וְעַל מַלְכוּת בֵּית דָּוִד מְשִׁיחֶךָ וְעַל הַבַּיִת הַגָּדוֹל וְהַקָּדוֹשׁ שֶׁנִּקְרָא שִׁמְךָ עָלָיו:

אֱלֹהֵינוּ אָבִינוּ, רְעֵנוּ זוּנֵנוּ פַּרְנְסֵנוּ וְכַלְכְּלֵנוּ וְהַרְוִיחֵנוּ, וְהַרְוַח לָנוּ ה' אֱלֹהֵינוּ מְהֵרָה מִכָּל צָרוֹתֵינוּ.

Please have mercy, Lord our God, upon Israel, Your people; and upon Jerusalem, Your city; and upon Zion, the dwelling place of Your Glory; and upon the monarchy of the House of David, Your appointed one; and upon the great and holy house that Your name is called upon. Our God, our Father, tend us, sustain us, provide for us, relieve us and give us quick relief, Lord our God, from all of our troubles.

For Discussion
We Pray Not to Need Handouts from Other Human Beings

וְנָא אַל תַּצְרִיכֵנוּ ה' אֱלֹהֵינוּ, לֹא לִידֵי מַתְּנַת בָּשָׂר וָדָם וְלֹא לִידֵי הַלְוָאָתָם, כִּי אִם לְיָדְךָ הַמְּלֵאָה הַפְּתוּחָה הַקְּדוֹשָׁה וְהָרְחָבָה, שֶׁלֹּא נֵבוֹשׁ וְלֹא נִכָּלֵם לְעוֹלָם וָעֶד.

Please do not make us, Lord our God, need the gifts of flesh and blood and not for their loans, but rather from Your full, open, holy and broad hand—so that we not be embarrassed, and we not be ashamed forever and always.

Judaism regards needing and taking money from others as an embarrassment. That is why virtually every early Jewish community in America founded a "free loan" (that is, interest-free) society—to enable Jews to meet fundamental needs such as food and lodging and to avoid receiving government help. To receive aid from the government was deemed a *shanda*, Yiddish for "shame." Of course, sometimes circumstances are such that there is no choice. However, we Jews pray not to need "the gifts of flesh and blood."

On Shabbat, add the following paragraph:

רְצֵה וְהַחֲלִיצֵנוּ ה' אֱלֹהֵינוּ בְּמִצְוֹתֶיךָ וּבְמִצְוַת יוֹם הַשְּׁבִיעִי הַשַּׁבָּת הַגָּדוֹל וְהַקָּדוֹשׁ הַזֶּה. כִּי יוֹם זֶה גָּדוֹל וְקָדוֹשׁ הוּא לְפָנֶיךָ לִשְׁבָּת בּוֹ וְלָנוּחַ בּוֹ בְּאַהֲבָה כְּמִצְוַת רְצוֹנֶךָ. וּבִרְצוֹנְךָ הָנִיחַ לָנוּ ה' אֱלֹהֵינוּ שֶׁלֹּא תְהֵא צָרָה וְיָגוֹן וַאֲנָחָה בְּיוֹם מְנוּחָתֵנוּ. וְהַרְאֵנוּ ה' אֱלֹהֵינוּ בְּנֶחָמַת צִיּוֹן עִירֶךָ וּבְבִנְיַן יְרוּשָׁלַיִם עִיר קָדְשֶׁךָ כִּי אַתָּה הוּא בַּעַל הַיְשׁוּעוֹת וּבַעַל הַנֶּחָמוֹת.

May You be pleased to embolden us, Lord our God, in Your commandments and in the command of the seventh day, of this great and holy Shabbat, since this day is great and holy before You, to cease work upon it and to rest upon it, with love, according to the commandment of Your will. And with Your will, allow us, Lord our God, that we should not have trouble, and grief and sighing on the day of our rest. And may You show us, Lord our God, the consolation of Zion, Your city; and the building of Jerusalem, Your holy city; since You are the Master of salvations and of consolations.

The following paragraph is added to the Birkat HaMazon only on holidays (the specific holiday is mentioned in it):

אֱלֹהֵינוּ וֵאלֹהֵי אֲבוֹתֵינוּ, יַעֲלֶה וְיָבֹא וְיַגִּיעַ וְיֵרָאֶה וְיֵרָצֶה וְיִשָּׁמַע וְיִפָּקֵד וְיִזָּכֵר זִכְרוֹנֵנוּ וּפִקְדוֹנֵנוּ, וְזִכְרוֹן אֲבוֹתֵינוּ, וְזִכְרוֹן מָשִׁיחַ בֶּן דָּוִד עַבְדֶּךָ, וְזִכְרוֹן יְרוּשָׁלַיִם עִיר קָדְשֶׁךָ, וְזִכְרוֹן כָּל עַמְּךָ בֵּית יִשְׂרָאֵל לְפָנֶיךָ, לִפְלֵיטָה לְטוֹבָה לְחֵן וּלְחֶסֶד וּלְרַחֲמִים, לְחַיִּים וּלְשָׁלוֹם בְּיוֹם חַג הַמַּצּוֹת הַזֶּה זָכְרֵנוּ ה' אֱלֹהֵינוּ בּוֹ לְטוֹבָה וּפָקְדֵנוּ בוֹ לִבְרָכָה וְהוֹשִׁיעֵנוּ בוֹ לְחַיִּים. וּבִדְבַר יְשׁוּעָה וְרַחֲמִים חוּס וְחָנֵּנוּ וְרַחֵם עָלֵינוּ וְהוֹשִׁיעֵנוּ, כִּי אֵלֶיךָ עֵינֵינוּ, כִּי אֵל מֶלֶךְ חַנּוּן וְרַחוּם אָתָּה.

God and God of our ancestors, may there ascend and come and reach and be seen and be acceptable and be heard and be recalled and be remembered—our remembrance and our recollection; and the remembrance of our ancestors; and the remembrance of the messiah, the son of David, Your servant; and the remembrance of Jerusalem, Your holy city; and the remembrance of all Your people, the house of Israel—in front of You, for survival, for good, for grace, and for kindness, and for mercy, for life and for peace on this day of the Festival of Matzahs. Remember us, Lord our God, on it for good and recall us on it for survival and save us on it for life, and by the word of salvation and mercy, pity and grace us and have mercy on us and save us, since our eyes are upon You, since You are a graceful and merciful Power.

וּבְנֵה יְרוּשָׁלַיִם עִיר הַקֹּדֶשׁ בִּמְהֵרָה בְיָמֵינוּ. בָּרוּךְ אַתָּה ה', בּוֹנֵה בְרַחֲמָיו יְרוּשָׁלָיִם. אָמֵן.

And may You build Jerusalem, the holy city, quickly and in our days. Blessed are You, Lord, who builds Jerusalem in His mercy. Amen.

בָּרוּךְ אַתָּה ה', אֱלֹהֵינוּ מֶלֶךְ הָעוֹלָם, הָאֵל אָבִינוּ מַלְכֵּנוּ אַדִּירֵנוּ בּוֹרְאֵנוּ גּוֹאֲלֵנוּ יוֹצְרֵנוּ קְדוֹשֵׁנוּ קְדוֹשׁ יַעֲקֹב רוֹעֵנוּ רוֹעֵה יִשְׂרָאֵל הַמֶּלֶךְ הַטּוֹב וְהַמֵּטִיב לַכֹּל שֶׁבְּכָל יוֹם וָיוֹם הוּא הֵטִיב, הוּא מֵטִיב, הוּא יֵיטִיב לָנוּ. הוּא גְמָלָנוּ הוּא גוֹמְלֵנוּ הוּא יִגְמְלֵנוּ לָעַד, לְחֵן וּלְחֶסֶד וּלְרַחֲמִים וּלְרֶוַח הַצָּלָה וְהַצְלָחָה, בְּרָכָה וִישׁוּעָה נֶחָמָה פַּרְנָסָה וְכַלְכָּלָה וְרַחֲמִים וְחַיִּים וְשָׁלוֹם וְכָל טוֹב, וּמִכָּל טוּב לְעוֹלָם עַל יְחַסְּרֵנוּ.

Blessed are You, Lord our God, King of the Universe, the Power, our Father, our King, our Mighty One, our Creator, our Redeemer, our Shaper, our Holy One, the Holy One of Jacob, our Shepherd, the Shepherd of Israel, the good King, Who does good to all, since on every single day He has done good, He does good, He will do good, to us; He has granted us, He grants us, He will grant us forever—in grace and in kindness, and in mercy, and in relief—rescue and success, blessing and salvation, consolation, provision and relief and mercy and life and peace and all good; and may we not lack any good ever.

הָרַחֲמָן הוּא יִמְלוֹךְ עָלֵינוּ לְעוֹלָם וָעֶד. הָרַחֲמָן הוּא יִתְבָּרַךְ בַּשָּׁמַיִם וּבָאָרֶץ. הָרַחֲמָן הוּא יִשְׁתַּבַּח לְדוֹר דּוֹרִים, וְיִתְפָּאַר בָּנוּ לָעַד וּלְנֵצַח נְצָחִים, וְיִתְהַדַּר בָּנוּ לָעַד וּלְעוֹלְמֵי עוֹלָמִים.

May the Merciful One reign over us forever and always. May the Merciful One be blessed in the heavens and in the earth. May the Merciful One be praised for all generations, and exalted among us forever and ever, and glorified among us always and infinitely for all infinities.

הָרַחֲמָן הוּא יְפַרְנְסֵנוּ בְּכָבוֹד.

May the Merciful One help us attain an honorable livelihood.

This is most obviously a prayer that we be able to sustain ourselves materially.

But this prayer emphasizes something else—that we sustain ourselves honorably. It is, after all, quite possible to provide for ourselves dishonorably—through cheating in business, for example. Thus, we pray that we engage in business transactions honorably.

The purpose of Jewish prayer is not primarily to ask God for things. It is to remind us regularly who we are and who we should be, about the greatness of God, and what type of life we should lead. The Hebrew word meaning "to pray," *l'hitpallel*, literally means "to examine oneself."

הָרַחֲמָן הוּא יִשְׁבּוֹר עֻלֵּנוּ מֵעַל צַוָּארֵנוּ, וְהוּא יוֹלִיכֵנוּ קוֹמְמִיּוּת לְאַרְצֵנוּ.

May the Merciful One break our yolk from upon our necks and bring us upright to our land.

This prayer, said by Jews every day for nearly 1,900 years, was answered in 1948, with the establishment of the State of Israel.

הָרַחֲמָן הוּא יִשְׁלַח לָנוּ בְּרָכָה מְרֻבָּה בַּבַּיִת הַזֶּה, וְעַל שֻׁלְחָן זֶה שֶׁאָכַלְנוּ עָלָיו. הָרַחֲמָן הוּא יִשְׁלַח לָנוּ אֶת אֵלִיָּהוּ הַנָּבִיא זָכוּר לַטּוֹב, וִיבַשֶּׂר לָנוּ בְּשׂוֹרוֹת טוֹבוֹת יְשׁוּעוֹת וְנֶחָמוֹת.

May the Merciful One send us multiple blessings, to this home and upon this table upon which we have eaten. May the Merciful One send us Elijah the prophet. May he be remembered for good and announce to us tidings of good, of salvation and of consolation.

> The purpose of Jewish prayer is not primarily to ask God for things. The Hebrew word meaning "to pray," l'hitpallel, *literally means "to examine oneself."*

הָרַחֲמָן הוּא יְבָרֵךְ אֶת בַּעְלִי/אִשְׁתִּי. הָרַחֲמָן הוּא יְבָרֵךְ אֶת [אָבִי מוֹרִי] בַּעַל הַבַּיִת הַזֶּה. וְאֶת [אִמִּי מוֹרָתִי] בַּעֲלַת הַבַּיִת הַזֶּה, אוֹתָם וְאֶת בֵּיתָם וְאֶת זַרְעָם וְאֶת כָּל אֲשֶׁר לָהֶם. אוֹתָנוּ וְאֶת כָּל אֲשֶׁר לָנוּ, כְּמוֹ שֶׁנִּתְבָּרְכוּ אֲבוֹתֵינוּ אַבְרָהָם יִצְחָק וְיַעֲקֹב בַּכֹּל מִכֹּל כֹּל, כֵּן יְבָרֵךְ אוֹתָנוּ כֻּלָּנוּ יַחַד בִּבְרָכָה שְׁלֵמָה, וְנֹאמַר, אָמֵן.

May the Merciful One bless my husband/my wife. May the Merciful One bless [my father, my teacher,] the master of this home and [my mother, my teacher,] the mistress of this home, they and their home and their offspring and everything that is theirs. Us and all that is ours, as were blessed Abraham, Isaac, and Jacob, in everything, from everything, with everything. So, too, should He bless us, all of us together, with a complete blessing and we shall say, Amen.

It is difficult to imagine that husbands who ask for God's blessing on their wives and wives who ask for God's blessing on their husbands every time they have a meal will not have a more harmonious marriage. It is likewise difficult to imagine that children who ask for God's blessings on their father and mother every time they have a meal will not treat their parents with greater respect.

In one's parents' house, one recites:

May the Merciful One bless my father, my teacher, the master of this house, and my mother my teacher, the lady of this house, them, their house, their family, and all that is theirs.

In one's own home, one recites:

May the Merciful One bless me, (my wife/my husband), us, our family, and all that is ours.

Guests at another's house recite:

May the Merciful One bless the master of this house, the lady of this house, them, their family, and all that is theirs.

בַּמָּרוֹם יְלַמְּדוּ עֲלֵיהֶם וְעָלֵינוּ זְכוּת שֶׁתְּהֵא לְמִשְׁמֶרֶת שָׁלוֹם. וְנִשָּׂא בְרָכָה מֵאֵת ה', וּצְדָקָה מֵאלֹהֵי יִשְׁעֵנוּ, וְנִמְצָא חֵן וְשֵׂכֶל טוֹב בְּעֵינֵי אֱלֹהִים וְאָדָם.

From above, may they advocate upon them and upon us merit, that should protect us in peace; and may we carry a blessing from the Lord and charity from the God of our salvation; and find grace and good understanding in the eyes of God and man.

We should aim to be well regarded by both God and our fellow human beings (in that order). Those who care only (or care more) about what people think of them will lack the courage to do what is right if it entails being unpopular. At the same time, unless it entails moral compromise, one should seek to be respected and even liked by fellow human beings.

בשבת: הָרַחֲמָן הוּא יַנְחִילֵנוּ יוֹם שֶׁכֻּלּוֹ שַׁבָּת וּמְנוּחָה לְחַיֵּי הָעוֹלָמִים. הָרַחֲמָן הוּא יַנְחִילֵנוּ יוֹם שֶׁכֻּלּוֹ טוֹב.

[On Shabbat:] May the Merciful One give us to inherit the day that will be completely Shabbat and rest in everlasting life. May the Merciful One give us to inherit the day that will be all good.

הָרַחֲמָן הוּא יְזַכֵּנוּ לִימוֹת הַמָּשִׁיחַ וּלְחַיֵּי הָעוֹלָם הַבָּא.

May the Merciful One give us merit for the times of the messiah and for life in the world to come.

The clear implication of this prayer is that the Messianic age and the afterlife are not identical. The Messianic age is in this world, and the afterlife is, as the term denotes, after this life. See the discussion on pages 37–39 regarding Judaism and the afterlife.

מִגְדּוֹל יְשׁוּעוֹת מַלְכּוֹ וְעֹשֶׂה חֶסֶד לִמְשִׁיחוֹ לְדָוִד וּלְזַרְעוֹ עַד עוֹלָם. עֹשֶׂה שָׁלוֹם בִּמְרוֹמָיו, הוּא יַעֲשֶׂה שָׁלוֹם עָלֵינוּ וְעַל כָּל יִשְׂרָאֵל וְאִמְרוּ, אָמֵן.

A tower of salvations is our King; may He do kindness with His messiah, with David and his offspring, forever (2 Samuel 22:51). The One who makes peace above, may He make peace upon us and upon all of Israel; and say, Amen.

יְראוּ אֶת ה' קְדֹשָׁיו, כִּי אֵין מַחְסוֹר לִירֵאָיו. כְּפִירִים רָשׁוּ וְרָעֵבוּ, וְדֹרְשֵׁי ה' לֹא יַחְסְרוּ כָל טוֹב. הוֹדוּ לַה' כִּי טוֹב כִּי לְעוֹלָם חַסְדּוֹ. פּוֹתֵחַ אֶת יָדֶךָ, וּמַשְׂבִּיעַ לְכָל חַי רָצוֹן. בָּרוּךְ הַגֶּבֶר אֲשֶׁר יִבְטַח בַּה', וְהָיָה ה' מִבְטַחוֹ.

Fear the Lord, [you] His holy ones, since there is nothing lacking for those that fear Him. Young lions may go without and hunger, but those that seek the Lord will not lack any good thing (Psalm 34:10–11). Thank the Lord, since He is good, since His kindness is forever (Psalm 118:1). You open Your hand and satisfy the will of all living things (Psalm 145:16). Blessed is the man that trusts in the Lord and the Lord is his security (Jeremiah 17:7).

נַעַר הָיִיתִי גַם זָקַנְתִּי, וְלֹא רָאִיתִי צַדִּיק נֶעֱזָב, וְזַרְעוֹ מְבַקֶּשׁ לָחֶם.

I was a youth and I have also aged and I have not seen a righteous man forsaken and his offspring seeking bread (Psalm 37:25).

Many moderns have raised objections to this verse from the Psalms. They find untenable the implicit claim that no righteous person is ever abandoned or has children who are so poor that they must beg for bread. As one must assume that the Psalmist (traditionally assumed to be King David) saw at least as much misery as we see in our time, it is doubtful this statement was meant to be taken literally. We can only conjecture as to what the writer had in mind. Perhaps the intent was to say that righteous people always perceive God's caring presence. In the view of Professor Gottlieb, "Our tradition does not regard verses like this as a promise, but rather as an encouragement to do the right thing."

ה' עֹז לְעַמּוֹ יִתֵּן, ה' יְבָרֵךְ אֶת עַמּוֹ בַשָּׁלוֹם.

The Lord will give His people strength. The Lord will bless His people with peace (Psalm 29:11).

Before God blesses people with peace, He will bless them with strength. It is a rule of life that weakness provokes violence. Both among individuals and nations, weakness invites attack.

The Birkat HaMazon has ended.

The Third Cup of Wine

Drink the third cup of wine, saying the blessing over wine.

בָּרוּךְ אַתָּה ה', אֱלֹהֵינוּ מֶלֶךְ הָעוֹלָם בּוֹרֵא פְּרִי הַגָּפֶן.

Blessed are You, Lord our God, King of the universe, Who creates the fruit of the vine.

(Baruch ata Adonai, Eloheinu melech ha'olam bo'rei pri ha'gafen.)

Opening the Door for Elijah

A fifth cup of wine that is not consumed is present on the Seder table. It is the "cup of Elijah." Jewish tradition holds that the biblical prophet Elijah will return to announce the redemption of the Jews and the coming of the Messiah. On Seder night, Jews open the door for Elijah and set aside a fifth cup of wine for him to drink.

Shlomo Telushkin, Joseph Telushkin's late father (a man I revered for his honesty, kindness, and scholarship), had an insightful observation as to why Elijah is the designated visitor in Jewish folklore at every Seder. After Elijah defeated in debate and in battle the priests of Ba'al, who had been brought into Israel by the evil Queen Jezebel, the queen sought to kill Elijah, whereupon he fled into the desert and spent forty days in solitude. During this time, Elijah cried out to God, "The Israelites have forsaken your covenant and . . . I alone am left" (I Kings 19:10).

He apparently believed he was the only God-believing Jew left on earth. However, God did not permit Elijah to wallow in self-pity and self-righteousness; God gave him new tasks and sent him on his way. Perhaps here, in Elijah's exaggerated condemnation of all other Jews, is the kernel of the reason for his many reappearances. He who sees himself as the last faithful Jew is fated to bear constant witness to the eternity of Israel. Thus, Elijah is present when every male Jewish newborn is brought into the covenant (a special chair known as the "Elijah chair" is present at every circumcision) and when every Jewish family celebrates the Seder (to this day, circumcision and the Seder remain the most widely observed Jewish rituals). Elijah stands in a long line of Jews who, in a moment of despair, erroneously prophesied the end of the Jewish people.

Pour the cup of Elijah and open the door.

שְׁפֹךְ חֲמָתְךָ אֶל־הַגּוֹיִם אֲשֶׁר לֹא יְדָעוּךָ וְעַל־מַמְלָכוֹת אֲשֶׁר בְּשִׁמְךָ לֹא קָרָאוּ. כִּי אָכַל אֶת־יַעֲקֹב וְאֶת־נָוֵהוּ הֵשַׁמּוּ. שְׁפָךְ־עֲלֵיהֶם זַעֲמֶךָ וַחֲרוֹן אַפְּךָ יַשִּׂיגֵם. תִּרְדֹּף בְּאַף וְתַשְׁמִידֵם מִתַּחַת שְׁמֵי ה'.

Pour your wrath upon the nations that did not know You and upon the kingdoms that did not call upon Your Name! Since they have consumed Jacob and laid waste his habitation (Psalm 79:6–7). Pour out Your fury upon them and the fierceness of Your anger shall reach them (Psalm 69:25)! You shall pursue them with anger and eradicate them from under the skies of the Lord (Lamentations 3:66).

This ancient prayer asking God to avenge Jewish suffering disturbs some modern Jews. As it has never led Jews to initiate violence against non-Jews, it is difficult to explain why it troubles them. Perhaps that question can be another topic of discussion at your Seder table.

הַלֵּל
Hallel (Psalms Part II)

Pour the fourth cup and complete the Hallel.

לֹא לָנוּ, ה', לֹא לָנוּ, כִּי לְשִׁמְךָ תֵּן כָּבוֹד, עַל חַסְדְּךָ עַל אֲמִתֶּךָ. לָמָּה יֹאמְרוּ הַגּוֹיִם אַיֵּה נָא אֱלֹהֵיהֶם. וֵאלֹהֵינוּ בַשָּׁמָיִם, כֹּל אֲשֶׁר חָפֵץ עָשָׂה. עֲצַבֵּיהֶם כֶּסֶף וְזָהָב מַעֲשֵׂה יְדֵי אָדָם. פֶּה לָהֶם וְלֹא יְדַבֵּרוּ, עֵינַיִם לָהֶם וְלֹא יִרְאוּ. אָזְנַיִם לָהֶם וְלֹא יִשְׁמָעוּ, אַף לָהֶם וְלֹא יְרִיחוּן. יְדֵיהֶם וְלֹא יְמִישׁוּן, רַגְלֵיהֶם וְלֹא יְהַלֵּכוּ, לֹא יֶהְגּוּ בִּגְרוֹנָם.

Not to us, not to us, but rather to Your name, give glory for Your kindness and for Your truth. Why should the nations say, "Where is their God?" But our God is in the heavens, all that He wanted, He has done. Their idols are silver and gold, the work of men's hands. They have a mouth but do not speak; they have eyes but do not see. They have ears but do not hear; they have a nose but do not smell. Hands, but they do not feel; feet, but do not walk; they do not make a peep from their throat (Psalm 115:1–7).

These verses from this psalm have a special place in my life and heart.

When the Soviet Union existed, almost no Soviet citizen was allowed to leave that country. But thanks to international pressure, some Soviet Jews were granted permission to leave if they had an official invitation from Israel. So, between 1948 and 1967, the Israeli government sent young Israelis into the Soviet Union to smuggle in Jewish religious items and to smuggle out the names of Jews who wanted to emigrate, should some Jewish emigration be allowed. After the Six-Day War in 1967, when the Soviet Union broke off diplomatic relations with Israel, the Israeli government began sending Jews from outside Israel. In 1969, when I was twenty-one years old, Israel sent me into the Soviet Union for four weeks—to Moscow, Leningrad (St. Petersburg), and Baku, Azerbaijan (which was then part of the Soviet Union). Knowing that my hotel room in Moscow was bugged, each morning I would knock on one of the walls in my room, say something in Russian, and then sing words from this psalm in Hebrew: "Their idols are silver and gold, the work of men's hands. They have a mouth but do not speak; they have eyes but do not see. They have ears but do not hear; they have a nose but do not smell. Hands, but they do not feel; feet, but do not walk; they do not make a peep from their throat."

The "idols" reference was, of course, to the ubiquitous statues of Lenin and the virtual worship of him. A very common phrase, taught to every Soviet child, was, "Lenin lived, Lenin lives, Lenin will live," a Sovietized version of the age-old Hebrew prayer, "God was, God is, God will be." (My hotel room scene was re-enacted by a young actor in the film *No Safe Spaces*.)

כְּמוֹהֶם יִהְיוּ עֹשֵׂיהֶם, כֹּל אֲשֶׁר בֹּטֵחַ בָּהֶם. יִשְׂרָאֵל בְּטַח בַּה', עֶזְרָם וּמָגִנָּם הוּא. בֵּית אַהֲרֹן בִּטְחוּ בַה', עֶזְרָם וּמָגִנָּם הוּא. יִרְאֵי ה' בִּטְחוּ בה', עֶזְרָם וּמָגִנָּם הוּא. ה' זְכָרָנוּ יְבָרֵךְ. יְבָרֵךְ אֶת בֵּית יִשְׂרָאֵל, יְבָרֵךְ אֶת בֵּית אַהֲרֹן, יְבָרֵךְ יִרְאֵי ה', הַקְּטַנִּים עִם הַגְּדֹלִים. יֹסֵף ה' עֲלֵיכֶם, עֲלֵיכֶם וְעַל בְּנֵיכֶם. בְּרוּכִים אַתֶּם לַיי עֹשֵׂה שָׁמַיִם וָאָרֶץ. הַשָּׁמַיִם שָׁמַיִם לַיי וְהָאָרֶץ נָתַן לִבְנֵי אָדָם. לֹא הַמֵּתִים יְהַלְלוּ יָהּ וְלֹא כָּל יֹרְדֵי דוּמָה. וַאֲנַחְנוּ נְבָרֵךְ יָהּ מֵעַתָּה וְעַד עוֹלָם. הַלְלוּיָהּ.

Like them will be their makers, all those that trust in them. Israel, trust in the Lord; their help and shield is He. House of Aaron, trust in the Lord; their help and shield is He. Those that fear the Lord, trust in the Lord; their help and shield is He. The Lord who remembers us, will bless; He will bless the House of Israel; He will bless the House of Aaron. He will bless those that fear the Lord, the small ones with the great ones. May the Lord bring increase to you, to you and to your children. Blessed are you to the Lord, the maker of the heavens and the earth. The heavens are the Lord's heavens, but the earth He has given to the children of man. It is not the dead that will praise the Lord, and not those that go down to silence. But we will bless the Lord from now and forever. Hallelujah! (Psalm 115:8–18).

אָהַבְתִּי כִּי יִשְׁמַע ה' אֶת קוֹלִי תַּחֲנוּנָי. כִּי הִטָּה אָזְנוֹ לִי וּבְיָמַי אֶקְרָא. אֲפָפוּנִי חֶבְלֵי מָוֶת וּמְצָרֵי שְׁאוֹל מְצָאוּנִי, צָרָה וְיָגוֹן אֶמְצָא. וּבְשֵׁם ה' אֶקְרָא: אָנָּא ה' מַלְּטָה נַפְשִׁי. חַנּוּן ה' וְצַדִּיק, וֵאלֹהֵינוּ מְרַחֵם. שֹׁמֵר פְּתָאִים ה', דַּלּוֹתִי וְלִי יְהוֹשִׁיעַ. שׁוּבִי נַפְשִׁי לִמְנוּחָיְכִי, כִּי ה' גָּמַל עָלָיְכִי. כִּי חִלַּצְתָּ נַפְשִׁי מִמָּוֶת, אֶת עֵינִי מִן דִּמְעָה, אֶת רַגְלִי מִדֶּחִי. אֶתְהַלֵּךְ לִפְנֵי ה' בְּאַרְצוֹת הַחַיִּים. הֶאֱמַנְתִּי כִּי אֲדַבֵּר, אֲנִי עָנִיתִי מְאֹד. אֲנִי אָמַרְתִּי בְחָפְזִי כָּל הָאָדָם כֹּזֵב.

I have loved the Lord since He hears my voice, my supplications. Since He inclined His ear to me—and in my days, I will call out. The pangs of death have encircled me and the straits of the pit have found me and I found grief. And in the name of the Lord I called, "Please Lord, spare my soul." Gracious is the Lord and righteous, and our God acts mercifully. The Lord watches over the simple; I was poor and He has saved me. Return, my soul to your tranquility, since the Lord has favored you. Since You have rescued my soul from death, my eyes from tears, my feet from stumbling. I will walk before the Lord in the lands of the living. I have trusted when I said, "I am very afflicted." I said in my haste, "All men are liars" (Psalms 116:1–11).

מָה אָשִׁיב לַה' כֹּל תַּגְמוּלוֹהִי עָלָי. כּוֹס יְשׁוּעוֹת אֶשָּׂא וּבְשֵׁם ה' אֶקְרָא. נְדָרַי לַה' אֲשַׁלֵּם נֶגְדָה נָּא לְכָל עַמּוֹ. יָקָר בְּעֵינֵי ה' הַמָּוְתָה לַחֲסִידָיו. אָנָּה ה' כִּי אֲנִי עַבְדֶּךָ, אֲנִי עַבְדְּךָ בֶּן אֲמָתֶךָ, פִּתַּחְתָּ לְמוֹסֵרָי. לְךָ אֶזְבַּח זֶבַח תּוֹדָה וּבְשֵׁם ה' אֶקְרָא. נְדָרַי לַה' אֲשַׁלֵּם נֶגְדָה נָּא לְכָל עַמּוֹ. בְּחַצְרוֹת בֵּית ה', בְּתוֹכֵכִי יְרוּשָׁלָיִם. הַלְלוּיָהּ.

What can I give back to the Lord for all that He has favored me? A cup of salvations I will raise up and I will call out in the name of the Lord. My vows to the Lord I will pay, now in front of His entire people. Precious in the eyes of the Lord is the death of His pious ones. Please Lord, since I am Your servant, the son of Your maidservant; You have opened my chains. To You will I offer a thanksgiving offering and I will call out in the name of the Lord. My vows to the Lord I will pay, now in front of His entire people. In the courtyards of the house of the Lord, in your midst, Jerusalem. Hallelujah! (Psalm 116:12–19).

הַלְלוּ אֶת ה' כָּל גּוֹיִם, שַׁבְּחוּהוּ כָּל הָאֻמִּים. כִּי גָבַר עָלֵינוּ חַסְדּוֹ, וֶאֱמֶת ה' לְעוֹלָם. הַלְלוּיָהּ. הוֹדוּ לַה' כִּי טוֹב כִּי לְעוֹלָם חַסְדּוֹ. יֹאמַר נָא יִשְׂרָאֵל כִּי לְעוֹלָם חַסְדּוֹ. יֹאמְרוּ נָא בֵית אַהֲרֹן כִּי לְעוֹלָם חַסְדּוֹ. יֹאמְרוּ נָא יִרְאֵי ה' כִּי לְעוֹלָם חַסְדּוֹ

Praise the name of the Lord, all nations; extol Him, all peoples. Since His kindness has overwhelmed us and the truth of the Lord is forever. Halleluyah! Thank the Lord, since He is good, since His kindness is forever. Let Israel now say, "Thank the Lord, since He is good, since His kindness is forever." Let the House of Aaron now say, "Thank the Lord, since He is good, since His kindness is forever." Let those that fear the Lord now say, "Thank the Lord, since He is good, since His kindness is forever." (Psalms 117–118:4).

מִן הַמֵּצַר קָרָאתִי יָּה, עָנָנִי בַמֶּרְחָב יָה. ה' לִי, לֹא אִירָא – מַה יַּעֲשֶׂה לִי אָדָם ה' לִי בְּעֹזְרָי וַאֲנִי אֶרְאֶה בְשֹׂנְאָי.

From the strait I have called, Lord; He answered me from the wide space, the Lord. The Lord is for me, I will not fear, what will man do to me? The Lord is for me with my helpers, and I shall glare at those that hate me (Psalm 118:5–7).

In the Hebrew Bible, the words God most often says to human beings are: "Do not fear." And the best way not to fear people is to fear God.

טוֹב לַחֲסוֹת בַּה' מִבְּטֹחַ בָּאָדָם. טוֹב לַחֲסוֹת בַּה' מִבְּטֹחַ בִּנְדִיבִים. כָּל גּוֹיִם סְבָבוּנִי, בְּשֵׁם ה' כִּי אֲמִילַם. סַבּוּנִי גַם סְבָבוּנִי, בְּשֵׁם ה' כִּי אֲמִילַם. סַבּוּנִי כִדְבֹרִים, דֹּעֲכוּ כְּאֵשׁ קוֹצִים, בְּשֵׁם ה' כִּי אֲמִילַם. דָּחֹה דְחִיתַנִי לִנְפֹּל, וַה' עֲזָרָנִי. עָזִּי וְזִמְרָת יָה וַיְהִי לִי לִישׁוּעָה. קוֹל רִנָּה וִישׁוּעָה בְּאָהֳלֵי צַדִּיקִים: יְמִין ה' עֹשָׂה חָיִל, יְמִין ה' רוֹמֵמָה, יְמִין ה' עֹשָׂה חָיִל. לֹא אָמוּת כִּי אֶחְיֶה, וַאֲסַפֵּר מַעֲשֵׂי יָה. יַסֹּר יִסְּרַנִי יָּה, וְלַמָּוֶת לֹא נְתָנָנִי. פִּתְחוּ לִי שַׁעֲרֵי צֶדֶק, אָבֹא בָם, אוֹדֶה יָהּ. זֶה הַשַּׁעַר לַה', צַדִּיקִים יָבֹאוּ בוֹ.

It is better to take refuge with the Lord than to trust in man. It is better to take refuge with the Lord than to trust in nobles. All the nations surrounded me; in the name of the Lord, I will chop them off. They surrounded me, they also encircled me; in the name of the Lord, I will chop them off. They surrounded me like bees, they were extinguished like a fire of thorns; in the name of the Lord, I will chop them off. You have surely pushed me to fall, but the Lord helped me. My boldness and song is the Lord, and He has become my salvation. The sound of happy song and salvation is in the tents of the righteous, the right hand of the Lord acts powerfully. I will not die but rather I will live and tell of the acts of the Lord. The Lord has surely chastised me, but He has not given me over to death. Open up for me the gates of righteousness; I will enter them, thank the Lord. This is the gate of the Lord; the righteous will enter it (Psalm 118:8–20).

אוֹדְךָ כִּי עֲנִיתָנִי וַתְּהִי לִי לִישׁוּעָה. אוֹדְךָ כִּי עֲנִיתָנִי וַתְּהִי לִי לִישׁוּעָה. אֶבֶן מָאֲסוּ
הַבּוֹנִים הָיְתָה לְרֹאשׁ פִּנָּה. אֶבֶן מָאֲסוּ הַבּוֹנִים הָיְתָה לְרֹאשׁ פִּנָּה. מֵאֵת ה' הָיְתָה
זֹּאת הִיא נִפְלָאת בְּעֵינֵינוּ. מֵאֵת ה' הָיְתָה זֹּאת הִיא נִפְלָאת בְּעֵינֵינוּ. זֶה הַיּוֹם
עָשָׂה ה'. נָגִילָה וְנִשְׂמְחָה בוֹ. זֶה הַיּוֹם עָשָׂה ה'. נָגִילָה וְנִשְׂמְחָה בוֹ.

*I will thank You, since You answered me and You have become my salvation. The stone
that was left by the builders has become the main cornerstone. From the Lord was this,
it is wondrous in our eyes. This is the day of the Lord, let us exult and rejoice upon it
(Psalm 118:21–24).*

אָנָּא ה', הוֹשִׁיעָה נָּא. אָנָּא ה', הוֹשִׁיעָה נָּא. אָנָּא ה', הַצְלִיחָה נָּא. אָנָּא ה',
הַצְלִיחָה נָּא.

Please, Lord, save us now; please, Lord, give us success now! (Psalm 118:25)

בָּרוּךְ הַבָּא בְּשֵׁם ה', בֵּרַכְנוּכֶם מִבֵּית ה'. בָּרוּךְ הַבָּא בְּשֵׁם ה', בֵּרַכְנוּכֶם מִבֵּית ה'.
אֵל ה' וַיָּאֶר לָנוּ. אִסְרוּ חַג בַּעֲבֹתִים עַד קַרְנוֹת הַמִּזְבֵּחַ. אֵל ה' וַיָּאֶר לָנוּ. אִסְרוּ
חַג בַּעֲבֹתִים עַד קַרְנוֹת הַמִּזְבֵּחַ. אֵלִי אַתָּה וְאוֹדֶךָּ, אֱלֹהַי – אֲרוֹמְמֶךָּ. אֵלִי אַתָּה
וְאוֹדֶךָּ, אֱלֹהַי – אֲרוֹמְמֶךָּ. הוֹדוּ לַיי כִּי טוֹב, כִּי לְעוֹלָם חַסְדּוֹ. הוֹדוּ לַיי כִּי טוֹב,
כִּי לְעוֹלָם חַסְדּוֹ.

*Blessed be the one who comes in the name of the Lord; we have blessed you from the
house of the Lord. God is the Lord, and He has illuminated us; tie up the festival offering with ropes until it reaches the corners of the altar. You are my Power and I will
thank You; my God and I will exalt You. Thank the Lord, since He is good, since His
kindness is forever (Psalm 118:26–29).*

יְהַלְלוּךָ ה' אֱלֹהֵינוּ כָּל מַעֲשֶׂיךָ, וַחֲסִידֶיךָ צַדִּיקִים עוֹשֵׂי רְצוֹנֶךָ, וְכָל עַמְּךָ בֵּית
יִשְׂרָאֵל בְּרִנָּה יוֹדוּ וִיבָרְכוּ, וִישַׁבְּחוּ וִיפָאֲרוּ, וִירוֹמְמוּ וְיַעֲרִיצוּ, וְיַקְדִּישׁוּ וְיַמְלִיכוּ
אֶת שִׁמְךָ, מַלְכֵּנוּ. כִּי לְךָ טוֹב לְהוֹדוֹת וּלְשִׁמְךָ נָאֶה לְזַמֵּר, כִּי מֵעוֹלָם וְעַד עוֹלָם
אַתָּה אֵל.

All of your works shall praise You, Lord our God, and your pious ones, the righteous ones who do Your will; and all of Your people, the House of Israel will thank and bless in joyful song: and extol and glorify, and exalt and acclaim, and sanctify and coronate Your name, our King. Since, You it is good to thank, and to Your name it is pleasant to sing, since from always and forever are You the Power.

Songs of Praise and Thanks

In the following prayer, each sentence ends with the words, "because His kindness is forever." At some Seders, the leader reads the first words of each sentence and the other participants respond, "because His kindness is forever." In Hebrew, the words are כִּי לְעוֹלָם חַסְדּוֹ (*ki l'olam chasdo*).

הוֹדוּ לַה' כִּי טוֹב

כִּי לְעוֹלָם חַסְדּוֹ.   הוֹדוּ לֵאלֹהֵי הָאֱלֹהִים

כִּי לְעוֹלָם חַסְדּוֹ.   הוֹדוּ לַאֲדֹנֵי הָאֲדֹנִים

כִּי לְעוֹלָם חַסְדּוֹ.   לְעֹשֵׂה נִפְלָאוֹת גְּדֹלוֹת לְבַדּוֹ

כִּי לְעוֹלָם חַסְדּוֹ.   לְעֹשֵׂה הַשָּׁמַיִם בִּתְבוּנָה

כִּי לְעוֹלָם חַסְדּוֹ.   לְרוֹקַע הָאָרֶץ עַל הַמָּיִם

כִּי לְעוֹלָם חַסְדּוֹ.   לְעֹשֵׂה אוֹרִים גְּדֹלִים

כִּי לְעוֹלָם חַסְדּוֹ.   אֶת הַשֶּׁמֶשׁ לְמֶמְשֶׁלֶת בַּיּוֹם

כִּי לְעוֹלָם חַסְדּוֹ.   אֶת הַיָּרֵחַ וְכוֹכָבִים לְמֶמְשְׁלוֹת בַּלָּיְלָה

כִּי לְעוֹלָם חַסְדּוֹ.   לְמַכֵּה מִצְרַיִם בִּבְכוֹרֵיהֶם

כִּי לְעוֹלָם חַסְדּוֹ.   וַיּוֹצֵא יִשְׂרָאֵל מִתּוֹכָם

כִּי לְעוֹלָם חַסְדּוֹ.   בְּיָד חֲזָקָה וּבִזְרוֹעַ נְטוּיָה

כִּי לְעוֹלָם חַסְדּוֹ.	לְגֹזֵר יַם סוּף לִגְזָרִים
כִּי לְעוֹלָם חַסְדּוֹ.	וְהֶעֱבִיר יִשְׂרָאֵל בְּתוֹכוֹ
כִּי לְעוֹלָם חַסְדּוֹ.	וְנִעֵר פַּרְעֹה וְחֵילוֹ בְיַם סוּף
כִּי לְעוֹלָם חַסְדּוֹ.	לְמוֹלִיךְ עַמּוֹ בַּמִּדְבָּר
כִּי לְעוֹלָם חַסְדּוֹ.	לְמַכֵּה מְלָכִים גְּדֹלִים
כִּי לְעוֹלָם חַסְדּוֹ.	וַיַּהֲרֹג מְלָכִים אַדִּירִים
כִּי לְעוֹלָם חַסְדּוֹ.	לְסִיחוֹן מֶלֶךְ הָאֱמֹרִי
כִּי לְעוֹלָם חַסְדּוֹ.	וּלְעוֹג מֶלֶךְ הַבָּשָׁן
כִּי לְעוֹלָם חַסְדּוֹ.	וְנָתַן אַרְצָם לְנַחֲלָה
כִּי לְעוֹלָם חַסְדּוֹ.	נַחֲלָה לְיִשְׂרָאֵל עַבְדּוֹ
כִּי לְעוֹלָם חַסְדּוֹ.	שֶׁבְּשִׁפְלֵנוּ זָכַר לָנוּ
כִּי לְעוֹלָם חַסְדּוֹ.	וַיִּפְרְקֵנוּ מִצָּרֵינוּ
כִּי לְעוֹלָם חַסְדּוֹ.	נֹתֵן לֶחֶם לְכָל בָּשָׂר
כִּי לְעוֹלָם חַסְדּוֹ.	הוֹדוּ לְאֵל הַשָּׁמָיִם

Thank the Lord, since He is good,

Thank the Power of powers,

To the Master of masters,

because His kindness is forever.

because His kindness is forever.

To the One who alone does wondrously great deeds,

because His kindness is forever.

To the one who made the Heavens with discernment,

because His kindness is forever.

To the One who spread the earth over the waters,

because His kindness is forever.

To the One who made great lights,

because His kindness is forever.

The sun to rule in the day,

because His kindness is forever.

The moon and the stars to rule in the night,

because His kindness is forever.

To the One that smote Egypt through their firstborn,

because His kindness is forever.

And He took Israel out from among them,

because His kindness is forever.

With a strong hand and an outstretched forearm,

because His kindness is forever.

To the One who cut up the Red Sea into strips,

because His kindness is forever.

And He made Israel to pass through it,

because His kindness is forever.

And He jolted Pharaoh and his troop in the Red Sea,

because His kindness is forever.

To the One who led his people in the wilderness,

because His kindness is forever.

To the One who smote great kings,

because His kindness is forever.

And he killed mighty kings,

because His kindness is forever.

Sichon, king of the Amorite,

because His kindness is forever.

And Og, king of the Bashan,

because His kindness is forever.

And he gave their land as an inheritance,

because His kindness is forever.

An inheritance for Israel, His servant,

because His kindness is forever.

That in our lowliness, He remembered us,

because His kindness is forever.

And he delivered us from our adversaries,

because His kindness is forever.

He gives bread to all flesh,

because His kindness is forever.

Thank the Power of the heavens,

because His kindness is forever.

(Psalm 136)

נִשְׁמַת כָּל חַי תְּבָרֵךְ אֶת שִׁמְךָ, ה' אֱלֹהֵינוּ, וְרוּחַ כָּל בָּשָׂר תְּפָאֵר וּתְרוֹמֵם זִכְרְךָ, מַלְכֵּנוּ, תָּמִיד. מִן הָעוֹלָם וְעַד הָעוֹלָם אַתָּה אֵל, וּמִבַּלְעָדֶיךָ אֵין לָנוּ מֶלֶךְ גּוֹאֵל וּמוֹשִׁיעַ, פּוֹדֶה וּמַצִּיל וּמְפַרְנֵס וּמְרַחֵם בְּכָל עֵת צָרָה וְצוּקָה. אֵין לָנוּ מֶלֶךְ אֶלָּא אָתָּה. אֱלֹהֵי הָרִאשׁוֹנִים וְהָאַחֲרוֹנִים, אֱלוֹהַּ כָּל בְּרִיּוֹת, אֲדוֹן כָּל תּוֹלָדוֹת, הַמְהֻלָּל בְּרֹב הַתִּשְׁבָּחוֹת, הַמְנַהֵג עוֹלָמוֹ בְּחֶסֶד וּבְרִיּוֹתָיו בְּרַחֲמִים. וַה' לֹא יָנוּם וְלֹא יִישָׁן — הַמְעוֹרֵר יְשֵׁנִים וְהַמֵּקִיץ נִרְדָּמִים, וְהַמֵּשִׂיחַ אִלְּמִים וְהַמַּתִּיר אֲסוּרִים וְהַסּוֹמֵךְ נוֹפְלִים וְהַזּוֹקֵף כְּפוּפִים. לְךָ לְבַדְּךָ אֲנַחְנוּ מוֹדִים.

The soul of every living being shall bless Your Name, Lord our God; the spirit of all flesh shall glorify and exalt Your remembrance always, our King. From the world and until the world, You are the Power, and other than You we have no king, redeemer, or savior, restorer, rescuer, provider, and merciful one in every time of distress and anguish; we have no king, besides You! God of the first ones and the last ones, God of all creatures, Master of all generations, Who is praised through a multitude of praises, Who guides His world with kindness and His creatures with mercy. The Lord neither slumbers nor sleeps. He who rouses the sleepers and awakens the dozers; He who makes the mute speak, and frees the captives, and supports the falling, and straightens the bent. We thank You alone.

אִלּוּ פִינוּ מָלֵא שִׁירָה כַיָּם, וּלְשׁוֹנֵנוּ רִנָּה כַּהֲמוֹן גַּלָּיו, וְשִׂפְתוֹתֵינוּ שֶׁבַח כְּמֶרְחֲבֵי
רָקִיעַ, וְעֵינֵינוּ מְאִירוֹת כַּשֶּׁמֶשׁ וְכַיָּרֵחַ, וְיָדֵינוּ פְרוּשׂוֹת כְּנִשְׁרֵי שָׁמַיִם, וְרַגְלֵינוּ
קַלּוֹת כָּאַיָּלוֹת – אֵין אֲנַחְנוּ מַסְפִּיקִים לְהוֹדוֹת לְךָ, ה' אֱלֹהֵינוּ וֵאלֹהֵי אֲבוֹתֵינוּ,
וּלְבָרֵךְ אֶת שְׁמֶךָ עַל אַחַת מֵאֶלֶף, אֶלֶף אַלְפֵי אֲלָפִים וְרִבֵּי רְבָבוֹת פְּעָמִים הַטּוֹבוֹת
שֶׁעָשִׂיתָ עִם אֲבוֹתֵינוּ וְעִמָּנוּ. מִמִּצְרַיִם גְּאַלְתָּנוּ, ה' אֱלֹהֵינוּ, וּמִבֵּית עֲבָדִים
פְּדִיתָנוּ, בְּרָעָב זַנְתָּנוּ וּבְשָׂבָע כִּלְכַּלְתָּנוּ, מֵחֶרֶב הִצַּלְתָּנוּ וּמִדֶּבֶר מִלַּטְתָּנוּ, וּמֵחֳלָיִם
רָעִים וְנֶאֱמָנִים דִּלִּיתָנוּ.

Were our mouth as full of song as the sea, and our tongue as full of joyous song as its multitude of waves, and our lips as full of praise as the breadth of the heavens, and our eyes as sparkling as the sun and the moon, and our hands as outspread as the eagles of the sky and our feet as swift as deer—we still could not thank You sufficiently, Lord our God and God of our ancestors, and to bless Your Name for one thousandth of the thousand of thousands of thousands, and myriad myriads, of goodnesses that You performed for our ancestors and for us. From Egypt, Lord our God, did You redeem us and from the house of slaves You restored us. In famine You nourished us, and in plenty You sustained us. From the sword You saved us, and from plague You spared us; and from severe and enduring diseases You delivered us.

עַד הֵנָּה עֲזָרוּנוּ רַחֲמֶיךָ וְלֹא עֲזָבוּנוּ חֲסָדֶיךָ, וְאַל תִּטְּשֵׁנוּ, ה' אֱלֹהֵינוּ, לָנֶצַח. עַל כֵּן
אֵבָרִים שֶׁפִּלַּגְתָּ בָּנוּ וְרוּחַ וּנְשָׁמָה שֶׁנָּפַחְתָּ בְּאַפֵּינוּ וְלָשׁוֹן אֲשֶׁר שַׂמְתָּ בְּפִינוּ – הֵן הֵם
יוֹדוּ וִיבָרְכוּ וִישַׁבְּחוּ וִיפָאֲרוּ וִירוֹמְמוּ וְיַעֲרִיצוּ וְיַקְדִּישׁוּ וְיַמְלִיכוּ אֶת שִׁמְךָ מַלְכֵּנוּ.
כִּי כָל פֶּה לְךָ יוֹדֶה, וְכָל לָשׁוֹן לְךָ תִשָּׁבַע, וְכָל בֶּרֶךְ לְךָ תִכְרַע, וְכָל קוֹמָה לְפָנֶיךָ
תִשְׁתַּחֲוֶה, וְכָל לְבָבוֹת יִירָאוּךָ, וְכָל קֶרֶב וּכְלָיוֹת יְזַמְּרוּ לִשְׁמֶךָ. כַּדָּבָר שֶׁכָּתוּב,
כָּל עַצְמוֹתַי תֹּאמַרְנָה, ה' מִי כָמוֹךָ מַצִּיל עָנִי מֵחָזָק מִמֶּנּוּ וְעָנִי וְאֶבְיוֹן מִגֹּזְלוֹ. מִי
יִדְמֶה לָּךְ וּמִי יִשְׁוֶה לָּךְ וּמִי יַעֲרָךְ לָךְ הָאֵל הַגָּדוֹל, הַגִּבּוֹר וְהַנּוֹרָא, אֵל עֶלְיוֹן, קֹנֵה
שָׁמַיִם וָאָרֶץ. נְהַלֶּלְךָ וּנְשַׁבֵּחֲךָ וּנְפָאֶרְךָ וּנְבָרֵךְ אֶת שֵׁם קָדְשֶׁךָ, כָּאָמוּר: לְדָוִד, בָּרְכִי
נַפְשִׁי אֶת ה', וְכָל קְרָבַי אֶת שֵׁם קָדְשׁוֹ. הָאֵל בְּתַעֲצֻמוֹת עֻזֶּךָ, הַגָּדוֹל בִּכְבוֹד שְׁמֶךָ,
הַגִּבּוֹר לָנֶצַח וְהַנּוֹרָא בְּנוֹרְאוֹתֶיךָ, הַמֶּלֶךְ הַיּוֹשֵׁב עַל כִּסֵּא רָם וְנִשָּׂא. שׁוֹכֵן עַד מָרוֹם
וְקָדוֹשׁ שְׁמוֹ. וְכָתוּב: רַנְּנוּ צַדִּיקִים בַּה', לַיְשָׁרִים נָאוָה תְהִלָּה. בְּפִי יְשָׁרִים תִּתְהַלָּל,
וּבְדִבְרֵי צַדִּיקִים תִּתְבָּרַךְ, וּבִלְשׁוֹן חֲסִידִים תִּתְרוֹמָם, וּבְקֶרֶב קְדוֹשִׁים תִּתְקַדָּשׁ.

*Until now Your mercy has helped us, and Your kindness has not forsaken us; and do
not abandon us, Lord our God, forever. Therefore, the limbs that You set within us
and the spirit and soul that You breathed into our nostrils, and the tongue that You
placed in our mouth—verily, they shall thank and bless and praise and glorify, and exalt
and revere, and sanctify and coronate Your name, our King. For every mouth shall offer
thanks to You; and every tongue shall swear allegiance to You; and every knee shall
bend to You; and every upright one shall prostrate himself before You; all hearts shall
fear You; and all innermost feelings and thoughts shall sing praises to Your name, as the
matter is written (Psalm 35:10), "All my bones shall say, 'Lord, who is like You? You
save the poor man from one who is stronger than he, the poor and destitute from the
one who would rob him.'" Who is similar to You and who is equal to You and who can
be compared to You, O great, strong and awesome Power, O highest Power, Creator of
the heavens and the earth? We shall praise and extol and glorify and bless Your holy
name, as it is stated (Psalm 103:1): "[A Psalm] of David. Bless the Lord, O my soul;
and all that is within me, His holy name." The Power, in Your powerful boldness; the
Great, in the glory of Your name; the Strong One forever; the King who sits on His
high and elevated throne. He who dwells always; lofty and holy is His name. And as it
is written (Psalms 33:10): "Sing joyfully to the Lord, righteous ones, praise is beautiful
from the upright." By the mouth of the upright You shall be praised; by the lips of
the righteous shall You be blessed; by the tongue of the devout shall You be exalted;
and among the holy shall You be sanctified.*

וּבְמַקְהֲלוֹת רִבְבוֹת עַמְּךָ בֵּית יִשְׂרָאֵל בְּרִנָּה יִתְפָּאֵר שִׁמְךָ, מַלְכֵּנוּ, בְּכָל דּוֹר וָדוֹר,
שֶׁכֵּן חוֹבַת כָּל הַיְצוּרִים לְפָנֶיךָ, ה' אֱלֹהֵינוּ וֵאלֹהֵי אֲבוֹתֵינוּ, לְהוֹדוֹת לְהַלֵּל
לְשַׁבֵּחַ, לְפָאֵר לְרוֹמֵם לְהַדֵּר לְבָרֵךְ, לְעַלֵּה וּלְקַלֵּס עַל כָּל דִּבְרֵי שִׁירוֹת וְתִשְׁבְּחוֹת
דָּוִד בֶּן יִשַׁי עַבְדְּךָ מְשִׁיחֶךָ.

*And in the assemblies of the myriads of Your people, the House of Israel, in joyous song
will Your name be glorified, our King, in each and every generation; as it is the duty of
all creatures, before You, Lord our God, and God of our ancestors, to thank, to praise,
to extol, to glorify, to exalt, to lavish, to bless, to raise high and to acclaim—beyond
the words of the songs and praises of David, the son of Yishai, Your servant, Your
anointed one.*

יִשְׁתַּבַּח שִׁמְךָ לָעַד מַלְכֵּנוּ, הָאֵל הַמֶּלֶךְ הַגָּדוֹל וְהַקָּדוֹשׁ בַּשָּׁמַיִם וּבָאָרֶץ, כִּי לְךָ נָאֶה, ה' אֱלֹהֵינוּ וֵאלֹהֵי אֲבוֹתֵינוּ, שִׁיר וּשְׁבָחָה, הַלֵּל וְזִמְרָה, עֹז וּמֶמְשָׁלָה, נֶצַח, גְּדֻלָּה וּגְבוּרָה, תְּהִלָּה וְתִפְאֶרֶת, קְדֻשָּׁה וּמַלְכוּת, בְּרָכוֹת וְהוֹדָאוֹת מֵעַתָּה וְעַד עוֹלָם. בָּרוּךְ אַתָּה ה', אֵל מֶלֶךְ גָּדוֹל בַּתִּשְׁבָּחוֹת, אֵל הַהוֹדָאוֹת, אֲדוֹן הַנִּפְלָאוֹת, הַבּוֹחֵר בְּשִׁירֵי זִמְרָה, מֶלֶךְ אֵל חֵי הָעוֹלָמִים.

May Your name be praised forever, our King, the Power, the Great and holy King—in the heavens and in the earth. Since for You it is pleasant—O Lord our God and God of our ancestors—song and lauding, praise and hymn, boldness and dominion, triumph, greatness and strength, psalm and splendor, holiness and kingship, blessings and thanksgivings, from now and forever. Blessed are You Lord, Power, King exalted through laudings, Power of Thanksgivings, Master of Wonders, who chooses the songs of hymn—King, Power of the life of the worlds.

The Fourth Cup of Wine

Make the following blessings over the fourth cup of wine:

בָּרוּךְ אַתָּה ה', אֱלֹהֵינוּ מֶלֶךְ הָעוֹלָם בּוֹרֵא פְּרִי הַגָּפֶן.

Blessed are You, Lord our God, King of the universe, Who creates the fruit of the vine.

(Baruch ata Adonai, Eloheinu melech ha'olam bo'rei pri ha'gafen.)

After drinking the wine, recite the following blessing:

בָּרוּךְ אַתָּה ה' אֱלֹהֵינוּ מֶלֶךְ הָעוֹלָם, עַל הַגֶּפֶן וְעַל פְּרִי הַגֶּפֶן, עַל תְּנוּבַת הַשָּׂדֶה
וְעַל אֶרֶץ חֶמְדָּה טוֹבָה וּרְחָבָה שֶׁרָצִיתָ וְהִנְחַלְתָּ לַאֲבוֹתֵינוּ לֶאֱכֹל מִפִּרְיָהּ וְלִשְׂבּוֹעַ
מִטּוּבָהּ. רַחֶם נָא ה' אֱלֹהֵינוּ עַל יִשְׂרָאֵל עַמֶּךָ וְעַל יְרוּשָׁלַיִם עִירֶךָ וְעַל צִיּוֹן מִשְׁכַּן
כְּבוֹדֶךָ וְעַל מִזְבְּחֶךָ וְעַל הֵיכָלֶךָ וּבְנֵה יְרוּשָׁלַיִם עִיר הַקֹּדֶשׁ בִּמְהֵרָה בְיָמֵינוּ וְהַעֲלֵנוּ
לְתוֹכָהּ וְשַׂמְּחֵנוּ וְרַצֵּה וְהַחֲלִיצֵנוּ בְּיוֹם בִּנְיָנָהּ וְנֹאכַל מִפִּרְיָהּ וְנִשְׂבַּע מִטּוּבָהּ
וּנְבָרֶכְךָ עָלֶיהָ בִּקְדֻשָּׁה וּבְטָהֳרָה [וּרְצֵה וְהַחֲלִיצֵנוּ בְּיוֹם הַשַּׁבָּת הַזֶּה] וְשַׂמְּחֵנוּ
בְּיוֹם חַג הַמַּצּוֹת הַזֶּה, כִּי אַתָּה ה' טוֹב וּמֵטִיב לַכֹּל, וְנוֹדֶה לְךָ עַל הָאָרֶץ וְעַל פְּרִי
הַגָּפֶן.
בָּרוּךְ אַתָּה ה', עַל הָאָרֶץ וְעַל פְּרִי הַגָּפֶן.

Blessed are You, Lord our God, King of the universe, for the vine and for the fruit of the vine; and for the bounty of the field; and for a desirable, good and broad land, which You wanted to give to our fathers, to eat from its fruit and to be satiated from its goodness. Please have mercy, Lord our God, upon Israel Your people; and upon Jerusalem, Your city: and upon Zion, the dwelling place of Your glory; and upon Your altar; and upon Your sanctuary; and build Jerusalem Your holy city quickly in our days, and bring us up into it and gladden us in its building; and we shall eat from its fruit, and be satiated from its goodness, and bless You in holiness and purity. [On Shabbat: And may you be pleased to embolden us on this Shabbat day] and gladden us on this day of the Festival of Matzahs. Since You, Lord, are good and do good to all, we thank You for the land and for the fruit of the vine.

Blessed are You, Lord, for the land and for the fruit of the vine.

נִרְצָה
NIRTZAH
Acceptance and Conclusion

Nirtzah means "acceptance." It is hoped that God has accepted our Seder and its prayers. This raises another fundamental question for those who think about God and religion.

For Discussion
Does God Answer Our Prayers?

The reality, as we humans see it, is that God *sometimes* answers those who call upon Him; only God knows why, when, and whom He answers.

It is both natural and theologically legitimate to make requests of God—to pray for one's health or the health of a loved one, for help in resisting evil, or with regard to any of the other myriad challenges and tragedies that confront us. But answering requests is not the primary role of God, and many people who believe it is will become disappointed and perhaps even alienated from God.

God's role is to teach us how to lead a moral and holy life; how to become close to Him; how to attain wisdom (hence the Torah and the rest of the Bible); to provide a guide for reducing man-made suffering in this life (the Ten Commandments, the rest of the Torah, and the Prophets); to provide ultimate justice in an afterlife; and to be with us when we suffer. He is most certainly there "when we call out to Him," as myriad people have experienced when they have suffered, but that does not mean—it cannot mean—that God answers all requests as we would wish.

But answering requests is not the primary role of God, and many people who believe it is will become disappointed and perhaps even alienated from God.

My belief system is predicated on being more concerned with what God wants from us than with what we want from God. This may not be fully emotionally satisfying. But I derive great comfort from simply believing that God is good and just. I also feel closest to God when I study the Torah—it is, after all, His revelation to us—and when trying to do what He wants me to do. Expecting God to give them what they want has led many religious people to feel disappointed in God and then abandon their faith. To paraphrase American president John F. Kennedy's famous comment in his inaugural address, "Ask not what you want from God, but what God wants from you."

חֲסַל סִדּוּר פֶּסַח כְּהִלְכָתוֹ, כְּכָל מִשְׁפָּטוֹ וְחֻקָּתוֹ. כַּאֲשֶׁר זָכִינוּ לְסַדֵּר אוֹתוֹ כֵּן נִזְכֶּה לַעֲשׂוֹתוֹ. זָךְ שׁוֹכֵן מְעוֹנָה, קוֹמֵם קְהַל עֲדַת מִי מָנָה. בְּקָרוֹב נַהֵל נִטְעֵי כַנָּה פְּדוּיִם לְצִיּוֹן בְּרִנָּה.

Completed is the Seder of Pesach according to its law, according to all its judgment and statute. Just as we have merited to arrange it, so too, may we merit to do [its sacrifice]. Pure One who dwells in the habitation, raise up the congregation of the community, which whom can count. Bring close, lead the plantings of the sapling, redeemed, to Zion in joy.

לְשָׁנָה הַבָּאָה בִּירוּשָׁלַיִם הַבְּנוּיָה

Next year, let us be in the rebuilt Jerusalem!

The Omer
The Counting and Blessing of Each Day between Passover and Shavuot

The Torah commands Jews to count the Omer, each day between Passover and Shavuot, the next of the three festivals in the Jewish calendar. Exactly seven weeks are counted—Shavuot is the Hebrew word for "weeks." Deuteronomy 16:9 states, "You shall count off seven weeks; start to count the seven weeks when the sickle is first put to the standing grain."

The counting and blessing of those forty-nine days means Passover and Shavuot are organically connected. From ancient times, Shavuot has commemorated the giving of the Torah at Mount Sinai. The Torah speaks of just the Ten Commandments being given at Sinai, but Judaism associates Sinai with the giving of the Torah as well.

The linkage between Passover and Shavuot is three-fold:

First, Moses repeatedly asked of Pharaoh, "Let My people go, that they may worship Me [God]." The Exodus fulfilled the first part of Moses's demand ("Let My people go"), and the revelation at Sinai fulfilled the second ("that they may worship Me").

Second, the connectedness of the two holidays is meant to teach that freedom is possible only with moral law. Free people must discipline themselves, or they will end up losing their freedom. Why? Because when people do not control themselves, they will end up having others control them. Criminals are the best example. Because they do not control themselves, society has to.

The founders of the United States well understood this fact of human nature. Reflecting on the document he helped write that established a limited form of government in order to maximize individual freedom, John Adams wrote: "Our Constitution was made only for a moral and religious People. It is wholly inadequate to the government of any other."[17] In the same vein, James Madison wrote that without "sufficient virtue among men for self-government . . . nothing less than the chains of despotism can restrain them from destroying and devouring one another."[18]

Third, the Exodus celebrates freedom from external bondage. Shavuot celebrates freedom from internal bondage. We either follow God's laws and control ourselves—our appetites and passions—or we end up being ruled by our appetites and passions.

The counting of the Omer begins on the second night of Passover:

> *We either follow God's laws and control ourselves—our appetites and passions—or we end up being ruled by our appetites and passions.*

בָּרוּךְ אַתָּה ה', אֱלֹהֵינוּ מֶלֶךְ הָעוֹלָם, אֲשֶׁר קִדְּשָׁנוּ בְּמִצְוֹתָיו וְצִוָּנוּ עַל סְפִירַת הָעֹמֶר. הַיּוֹם יוֹם אֶחָד בָּעֹמֶר.

Blessed are You, Lord our God, King of the Universe, Who has sanctified us with His commandments and has commanded us on the counting of the omer. Today is the first day of the omer.

Barukh ata Adonai Eloheinu Melekh ha'Olam asher kid'shanu b'mitzvotav v'tizivanu al sefirat ha'omer. Ha-yom yom e-chad la-omer.

The following liturgical poem—"And It Happened at Midnight"—was composed around the sixth century. It is based on an ancient Jewish teaching that "all miracles performed for Israel, within which evildoers were punished, took place at night."[19] It is said on the first night of Passover. The poem's verses are arranged in Hebrew alphabetical order, common in liturgical poetry (for example, Psalm 145).

וַיְהִי בַּחֲצִי הַלַּיְלָה
"And It Happened at Midnight"

וּבְכֵן וַיְהִי בַּחֲצִי הַלַּיְלָה אָז רוֹב נִסִּים הִפְלֵאתָ בַּלַּיְלָה, בְּרֹאשׁ אַשְׁמוּרֶת זֶה הַלַּיְלָה, גֵּר צֶדֶק נִצַּחְתּוֹ כְּנֶחֱלַק לוֹ לַיְלָה, וַיְהִי בַּחֲצִי הַלַּיְלָה. דַּנְתָּ מֶלֶךְ גְּרָר בַּחֲלוֹם הַלַּיְלָה, הִפְחַדְתָּ אֲרַמִּי בְּאֶמֶשׁ לַיְלָה, וַיָּשַׂר יִשְׂרָאֵל לְמַלְאָךְ וַיּוּכַל לוֹ לַיְלָה, וַיְהִי בַּחֲצִי הַלַּיְלָה. זֶרַע בְּכוֹרֵי פַתְרוֹס מָחַצְתָּ בַּחֲצִי הַלַּיְלָה, חֵילָם לֹא מָצְאוּ בְּקוּמָם בַּלַּיְלָה, טִיסַת נְגִיד חֲרֹשֶׁת סִלִּיתָ בְּכוֹכְבֵי לַיְלָה, וַיְהִי בַּחֲצִי הַלַּיְלָה יָעַץ מְחָרֵף לְנוֹפֵף אִוּוּי, הוֹבַשְׁתָּ פְגָרָיו בַּלַּיְלָה, כָּרַע בֵּל וּמַצָּבוֹ בְּאִישׁוֹן לַיְלָה, לְאִישׁ חֲמוּדוֹת נִגְלָה רָז חֲזוֹת לַיְלָה, וַיְהִי בַּחֲצִי הַלַּיְלָה. מִשְׁתַּכֵּר בִּכְלֵי קֹדֶשׁ נֶהֱרַג בּוֹ בַּלַּיְלָה, נוֹשַׁע מִבּוֹר אֲרָיוֹת פּוֹתֵר בְּעִתּוּתֵי לַיְלָה, שִׂנְאָה נָטַר אֲגָגִי וְכָתַב סְפָרִים בַּלַּיְלָה, וַיְהִי בַּחֲצִי הַלַּיְלָה. עוֹרַרְתָּ נִצְחֲךָ עָלָיו בְּנֶדֶד שְׁנַת לַיְלָה. פּוּרָה תִדְרוֹךְ לְשׁוֹמֵר מַה מִּלַּיְלָה, צָרַח כַּשּׁוֹמֵר וְשָׂח אָתָא בֹקֶר וְגַם לַיְלָה, וַיְהִי בַּחֲצִי הַלַּיְלָה. קָרֵב יוֹם אֲשֶׁר הוּא לֹא יוֹם וְלֹא לַיְלָה, רָם הוֹדַע כִּי לְךָ הַיּוֹם אַף לְךָ הַלַּיְלָה, שׁוֹמְרִים הַפְקֵד לְעִירְךָ כָּל הַיּוֹם וְכָל הַלַּיְלָה, תָּאִיר כְּאוֹר יוֹם חֶשְׁכַּת לַיְלָה, וַיְהִי בַּחֲצִי הַלַּיְלָה.

And so, it was in the middle of the night. Then, most of the miracles did You wondrously do at night, at the first of the watches this night. A righteous convert did you make victorious when it was divided for him at night [referring to Abraham in his war against the four kings in Genesis 14:15], and it was in the middle of the night. You judged the king of Gerrar [Abimelekh] in a dream of the night; You frightened an Aramean [Laban] in the dark of the night; and Israel dominated an angel and was able to withstand Him at night [Genesis 32:25–30], and it was in the middle of the night. You crushed the firstborn of Patros [Pharaoh, as per Ezekiel 30:14] in the middle of the night, their wealth they did not find when they got up at night; the attack of the leader Charoshet [Sisera] did you sweep away by the stars of the night [Judges 5:20], and it was in the middle of the night. The blasphemer [Sennacherib, whose servants blasphemed when trying to discourage the inhabitants of Jerusalem] counseled to wave off the desired ones, You made him wear his corpses on his head at night (II Kings 19:35); Bel and his pedestal were bent in the pitch of night [in Nebuchadnezzar's dream in Daniel 2]; to the man of delight [Daniel] was revealed the secret visions at night, and it was in the middle of the night.

The one who got drunk [Belshazzar] from the holy vessels was killed on that night [Daniel 5:30], the one saved from the pit of lions [Daniel] interpreted the scary visions of the night; hatred was preserved by the Agagite [Haman] and he wrote books at night, and it was in the middle of the night (Esther 2:23). You aroused your victory upon him by disturbing the sleep of night [of King Achashverosh] (Esther 6:1), You will stomp the wine press for the one who guards from anything at night [Esau/Seir as per Isaiah 21:11]; He yelled like a guard and spoke, "The morning has come and also the night," and it was in the middle of the night. Bring close the day which is not day and not night [referring to the end of days in Zechariah 14:7], High One, make known that Yours is the day and also Yours is the night, guards appoint for Your city all the day and all the night, illuminate like the light of the day, the darkness of the night, and it was in the middle of the night.

Outside of Israel, where a second Seder is traditionally observed, the following poem is recited. Also written around the sixth century, it outlines the many historical events that the poet believed occurred during the Passover holiday. This poem, too, follows the order of the Hebrew alphabet.

וַאֲמַרְתֶּם זֶבַח פֶּסַח
"And You Shall Say, 'It Is the Pesach Sacrifice'"

אֹמֶץ גְּבוּרוֹתֶיךָ הִפְלֵאתָ בַּפֶּסַח, בְּרֹאשׁ כָּל מוֹעֲדוֹת נִשֵּׂאתָ פֶּסַח. גִּלִּיתָ לְאֶזְרָחִי חֲצוֹת לֵיל פֶּסַח, וַאֲמַרְתֶּם זֶבַח פֶּסַח. דְּלָתָיו דָּפַקְתָּ כְּחֹם הַיּוֹם בַּפֶּסַח, הִסְעִיד נוֹצְצִים עֻגוֹת מַצּוֹת בַּפֶּסַח, וְאֶל הַבָּקָר רָץ זֵכֶר לְשׁוֹר עֵרֶךְ פֶּסַח, וַאֲמַרְתֶּם זֶבַח פֶּסַח. זוֹעֲמוּ סְדוֹמִים וְלוֹהֲטוּ בָּאֵשׁ בַּפֶּסַח, חֻלַּץ לוֹט מֵהֶם וּמַצּוֹת אָפָה בְּקֵץ פֶּסַח, טִאטֵאתָ אַדְמַת מוֹף וְנוֹף בְּעָבְרְךָ בַּפֶּסַח. וַאֲמַרְתֶּם זֶבַח פֶּסַח. יָהּ רֹאשׁ כָּל הוֹן מָחַצְתָּ בְּלֵיל שִׁמּוּר פֶּסַח, כַּבִּיר, עַל בֵּן בְּכוֹר פָּסַחְתָּ בְּדַם פֶּסַח, לְבִלְתִּי תֵּת מַשְׁחִית לָבֹא בִּפְתָחַי בַּפֶּסַח, וַאֲמַרְתֶּם זֶבַח פֶּסַח. מְסֻגֶּרֶת סֻגָּרָה בְּעִתּוֹתֵי פֶּסַח, נִשְׁמְדָה מִדְיָן בִּצְלִיל שְׂעוֹרֵי עֹמֶר פֶּסַח, שׂוֹרָפוּ מִשְׁמַנֵּי פּוּל וְלוּד בִּיקַד יְקוֹד פֶּסַח, וַאֲמַרְתֶּם זֶבַח פֶּסַח. עוֹד הַיּוֹם בְּנֹב לַעֲמוֹד עַד גָּעָה עוֹנַת פֶּסַח, פַּס יַד כָּתְבָה לְקַעֲקֵעַ צוּל בַּפֶּסַח, צָפֹה הַצָּפִית עָרוֹךְ הַשֻּׁלְחָן בַּפֶּסַח, וַאֲמַרְתֶּם זֶבַח פֶּסַח. קָהָל כִּנְּסָה הֲדַסָּה לְשַׁלֵּשׁ צוֹם בַּפֶּסַח, רֹאשׁ מִבֵּית רָשָׁע מָחַצְתָּ בְּעֵץ חֲמִשִּׁים בַּפֶּסַח, שְׁתֵּי אֵלֶּה רֶגַע תָּבִיא לְעוּצִית בַּפֶּסַח, תָּעֹז יָדְךָ תָּרוּם יְמִינְךָ כְּלֵיל הִתְקַדֵּשׁ חַג פֶּסַח, וַאֲמַרְתֶּם זֶבַח פֶּסַח.

"And you shall say, 'It is the Pesach sacrifice'" (Exodus 12:27).

The boldness of Your strong deeds did you wondrously show at Pesach; at the head of all the holidays did You raise Pesach; You revealed to the Ezrachite [Abraham], midnight of the night of Pesach. "And you shall say, 'It is the Pesach sacrifice.'"

Upon his doors did You knock at the heat of the day on Pesach [Genesis 18:1]; he sustained shining ones [angels] with cakes of matzah on Pesach; and to the cattle he ran, in commemoration of the bull that was set up for Pesach. "And you shall say, 'It is the Pesach sacrifice.'"

The Sodomites caused Him indignation and He set them on fire on Pesach; Lot was rescued from them and matzahs did he bake at the end of Pesach; He swept the land of Mof and Nof [cities in Egypt] on Pesach. "And you shall say, 'It is the Pesach sacrifice.'"

The head of every firstborn did You crush on the guarded night of Pesach; Powerful One, over the firstborn son did You pass over with the blood on Pesach; so as to not let the destroyer come into my gates on Pesach. "And you shall say, 'It is the Pesach sacrifice.'"

The enclosed one [Jericho] was enclosed in the season of Pesach; Midian was destroyed with a portion of the omer-barley on Pesach [via Gideon as per Judges 7]; from the fat of Pul and Lud [Assyrian soldiers of Sennacherib] was burnt in pyres on Pesach. "And you shall say, 'It is the Pesach sacrifice.'"

Still today, [Sennacherib will go no further than] to stand in Nov [Isaiah 10:32], until he cried at the time of Pesach; a palm of the hand wrote [Daniel 5:5] to rip up the deep one [the Babylonian one, Belshazzar] on Pesach; set up the watch, set the table [referring to Balthasar, based on Isaiah 21:5] on Pesach. "And you shall say, 'It is the Pesach sacrifice.'"

The congregation did Hadassah [Esther] bring in to triple a fast on Pesach; the head of the house of evil [Haman] did you crush on a tree of fifty [cubits/amot] on Pesach; these two [plagues as per Isaiah 47:9] will you bring in an instant to the Utsi [Esau] on Pesach; embolden Your hand, raise Your right hand, as on the night You were sanctified on the festival of Pesach. "And you shall say, 'It is the Pesach sacrifice.'"

The Four Last Songs

In theory, the Passover Seder is now over. But few Seders end prior to singing the following four songs, some of whose melodies are among the most beautiful in Jewish music.

כִּי לוֹ נָאֶה
Ki Lo Na-eh
Since for Him It Is Pleasant

כִּי לוֹ נָאֶה, כִּי לוֹ יָאֶה.

אַדִּיר בִּמְלוּכָה, בָּחוּר כַּהֲלָכָה, גְּדוּדָיו יֹאמְרוּ לוֹ: לְךָ וּלְךָ, לְךָ כִּי לְךָ, לְךָ אַף לְךָ, לְךָ ה' הַמַּמְלָכָה, כִּי לוֹ נָאֶה, כִּי לוֹ יָאֶה.

דָּגוּל בִּמְלוּכָה, הָדוּר כַּהֲלָכָה, וָתִיקָיו יֹאמְרוּ לוֹ: לְךָ וּלְךָ, לְךָ כִּי לְךָ, לְךָ אַף לְךָ, לְךָ ה' הַמַּמְלָכָה, כִּי לוֹ נָאֶה, כִּי לוֹ יָאֶה.

זַכַּאי בִּמְלוּכָה, חָסִין כַּהֲלָכָה טַפְסְרָיו יֹאמְרוּ לוֹ: לְךָ וּלְךָ, לְךָ כִּי לְךָ, לְךָ אַף לְךָ, לְךָ ה' הַמַּמְלָכָה, כִּי לוֹ נָאֶה, כִּי לוֹ יָאֶה.

יָחִיד בִּמְלוּכָה, כַּבִּיר כַּהֲלָכָה לִמּוּדָיו יֹאמְרוּ לוֹ: לְךָ וּלְךָ, לְךָ כִּי לְךָ, לְךָ אַף לְךָ, לְךָ ה' הַמַּמְלָכָה, כִּי לוֹ נָאֶה, כִּי לוֹ יָאֶה.

מוֹשֵׁל בִּמְלוּכָה, נוֹרָא כַּהֲלָכָה סְבִיבָיו יֹאמְרוּ לוֹ: לְךָ וּלְךָ, לְךָ כִּי לְךָ, לְךָ אַף לְךָ, לְךָ ה' הַמַּמְלָכָה, כִּי לוֹ נָאֶה, כִּי לוֹ יָאֶה.

עָנָיו בִּמְלוּכָה, פּוֹדֶה כַּהֲלָכָה, צַדִּיקָיו יֹאמְרוּ לוֹ: לְךָ וּלְךָ, לְךָ כִּי לְךָ, לְךָ אַף לְךָ, לְךָ ה' הַמַּמְלָכָה, כִּי לוֹ נָאֶה, כִּי לוֹ יָאֶה.

קָדוֹשׁ בִּמְלוּכָה, רַחוּם כַּהֲלָכָה שִׁנְאַנָּיו יֹאמְרוּ לוֹ: לְךָ וּלְךָ, לְךָ כִּי לְךָ, לְךָ אַף לְךָ, לְךָ ה' הַמַּמְלָכָה, כִּי לוֹ נָאֶה, כִּי לוֹ יָאֶה.

תַּקִּיף בִּמְלוּכָה, תּוֹמֵךְ כַּהֲלָכָה תְּמִימָיו יֹאמְרוּ לוֹ: לְךָ וּלְךָ, לְךָ כִּי לְךָ, לְךָ אַף לְךָ, לְךָ ה' הַמַּמְלָכָה, כִּי לוֹ נָאֶה, כִּי לוֹ יָאֶה.

Since for Him it is pleasant, for Him it is suited.

Mighty in rulership, properly chosen, his troops shall say to Him, "Yours and Yours, Yours since it is Yours, Yours and even Yours, Yours, Lord is the kingdom; since for Him it is pleasant, for Him it is suited."

Noted in rulership, properly splendid, His distinguished ones will say to him, "Yours and Yours, Yours since it is Yours, Yours and even Yours, Yours, Lord is the kingdom; since for Him it is pleasant, for Him it is suited."

Meritorious in rulership, properly robust, His scribes shall say to him, "Yours and Yours, Yours since it is Yours, Yours and even Yours, Yours, Lord is the kingdom; since for Him it is pleasant, for Him it is suited."

Unique in rulership, properly powerful, His wise ones say to Him, "Yours and Yours, Yours since it is Yours, Yours and even Yours, Yours, Lord is the kingdom; since for Him it is pleasant, for Him it is suited."

Reigning in rulership, properly awesome, those around Him say to Him, "Yours and Yours, Yours since it is Yours, Yours and even Yours, Yours, Lord is the kingdom; since for Him it is pleasant, for Him it is suited."

Humble in rulership, properly restoring, His righteous ones say to Him, "Yours and Yours, Yours since it is Yours, Yours and even Yours, Yours, Lord is the kingdom; since for Him it is pleasant, for Him it is suited."

Holy in rulership, properly merciful, His angels say to Him, "Yours and Yours, Yours since it is Yours, Yours and even Yours, Yours, Lord is the kingdom; since for Him it is pleasant, for Him it is suited."

Dynamic in rulership, properly supportive, His innocent ones say to Him, "Yours and Yours, Yours since it is Yours, Yours and even Yours, Yours, Lord is the kingdom; since for Him it is pleasant, for Him it is suited."

אַדִּיר הוּא
Adir Hu
Mighty Is He

אַדִּיר הוּא יִבְנֶה בֵיתוֹ בְּקָרוֹב. בִּמְהֵרָה, בִּמְהֵרָה, בְּיָמֵינוּ בְּקָרוֹב. אֵל בְּנֵה, אֵל בְּנֵה, בְּנֵה בֵיתְךָ בְּקָרוֹב.

בָּחוּר הוּא, גָּדוֹל הוּא, דָּגוּל הוּא יִבְנֶה בֵיתוֹ בְּקָרוֹב. בִּמְהֵרָה, בִּמְהֵרָה, בְּיָמֵינוּ בְּקָרוֹב. אֵל בְּנֵה, אֵל בְּנֵה, בְּנֵה בֵיתְךָ בְּקָרוֹב.

הָדוּר הוּא, וָתִיק הוּא, זַכַּאי הוּא יִבְנֶה בֵיתוֹ בְּקָרוֹב. בִּמְהֵרָה, בִּמְהֵרָה, בְּיָמֵינוּ בְּקָרוֹב. אֵל בְּנֵה, אֵל בְּנֵה, בְּנֵה בֵיתְךָ בְּקָרוֹב.

חָסִיד הוּא, טָהוֹר הוּא, יָחִיד הוּא יִבְנֶה בֵיתוֹ בְּקָרוֹב. בִּמְהֵרָה, בִּמְהֵרָה, בְּיָמֵינוּ
בְּקָרוֹב. אֵל בְּנֵה, אֵל בְּנֵה, בְּנֵה בֵיתְךָ בְּקָרוֹב.
כַּבִּיר הוּא, לָמוּד הוּא, מֶלֶךְ הוּא יִבְנֶה בֵיתוֹ בְּקָרוֹב. בִּמְהֵרָה, בִּמְהֵרָה, בְּיָמֵינוּ
בְּקָרוֹב. אֵל בְּנֵה, אֵל בְּנֵה, בְּנֵה בֵיתְךָ בְּקָרוֹב.
נוֹרָא הוּא, סַגִּיב הוּא, עִזּוּז הוּא יִבְנֶה בֵיתוֹ בְּקָרוֹב. בִּמְהֵרָה, בִּמְהֵרָה, בְּיָמֵינוּ
בְּקָרוֹב. אֵל בְּנֵה, אֵל בְּנֵה, בְּנֵה בֵיתְךָ בְּקָרוֹב.
פּוֹדֶה הוּא, צַדִּיק הוּא, קָדוֹשׁ הוּא יִבְנֶה בֵיתוֹ בְּקָרוֹב. בִּמְהֵרָה, בִּמְהֵרָה, בְּיָמֵינוּ
בְּקָרוֹב. אֵל בְּנֵה, אֵל בְּנֵה, בְּנֵה בֵיתְךָ בְּקָרוֹב.
רַחוּם הוּא, שַׁדַּי הוּא, תַּקִּיף הוּא יִבְנֶה בֵיתוֹ בְּקָרוֹב. בִּמְהֵרָה, בִּמְהֵרָה, בְּיָמֵינוּ
בְּקָרוֹב. אֵל בְּנֵה, אֵל בְּנֵה, בְּנֵה בֵיתְךָ בְּקָרוֹב.

Mighty is He, may He build His house soon. Quickly, quickly, in our days, soon. God build, God build, build Your house soon.

Chosen is He, great is He, noted is He. Quickly, quickly, in our days, soon. God build, God build, build Your house soon.

Splendid is He, distinguished is He, meritorious is He. Quickly, quickly, in our days, soon. God build, God build, build Your house soon.

Pious is He, pure is He, unique is He. Quickly, quickly, in our days, soon. God build, God build, build Your house soon.

Powerful is He, wise is He, a King is He. Quickly, quickly, in our days, soon. God build, God build, build Your house soon.

Awesome is He, exalted is He, heroic is He. Quickly, quickly, in our days, soon. God build, God build, build Your house soon.

A restorer is He, righteous is He, holy is He. Quickly, quickly, in our days, soon. God build, God build, build Your house soon.

Merciful is He, the Omnipotent is He, dynamic is He. Quickly, quickly, in our days, soon. God build, God build, build Your house soon.

אֶחָד מִי יוֹדֵעַ?

Echad Mi Yodea

Who Knows One?

This song is a superb example of the educational nature of the Seder. Thanks to this song, which I sang from early childhood on, I could immediately tell you the number of patriarchs and matriarchs. This song works in English as well as it does in Hebrew.

אֶחָד מִי יוֹדֵעַ? אֶחָד אֲנִי יוֹדֵעַ: אֶחָד אֱלֹהֵינוּ שֶׁבַּשָּׁמַיִם וּבָאָרֶץ.

שְׁנַיִם מִי יוֹדֵעַ? שְׁנַיִם אֲנִי יוֹדֵעַ: שְׁנֵי לֻחוֹת הַבְּרִית. אֶחָד אֱלֹהֵינוּ שֶׁבַּשָּׁמַיִם וּבָאָרֶץ.

שְׁלֹשָׁה מִי יוֹדֵעַ? שְׁלֹשָׁה אֲנִי יוֹדֵעַ: שְׁלֹשָׁה אָבוֹת, שְׁנֵי לֻחוֹת הַבְּרִית, אֶחָד אֱלֹהֵינוּ שֶׁבַּשָּׁמַיִם וּבָאָרֶץ.

אַרְבַּע מִי יוֹדֵעַ? אַרְבַּע אֲנִי יוֹדֵעַ: אַרְבַּע אִמָּהוֹת, שְׁלֹשָׁה אָבוֹת, שְׁנֵי לֻחוֹת הַבְּרִית, אֶחָד אֱלֹהֵינוּ שֶׁבַּשָּׁמַיִם וּבָאָרֶץ.

חֲמִשָּׁה מִי יוֹדֵעַ? חֲמִשָּׁה אֲנִי יוֹדֵעַ: חֲמִשָּׁה חוּמְשֵׁי תוֹרָה, אַרְבַּע אִמָּהוֹת, שְׁלֹשָׁה אָבוֹת, שְׁנֵי לֻחוֹת הַבְּרִית, אֶחָד אֱלֹהֵינוּ שֶׁבַּשָּׁמַיִם וּבָאָרֶץ.

שִׁשָּׁה מִי יוֹדֵעַ? שִׁשָּׁה אֲנִי יוֹדֵעַ: שִׁשָּׁה סִדְרֵי מִשְׁנָה, חֲמִשָּׁה חוּמְשֵׁי תוֹרָה, אַרְבַּע אִמָּהוֹת, שְׁלֹשָׁה אָבוֹת, שְׁנֵי לֻחוֹת הַבְּרִית, אֶחָד אֱלֹהֵינוּ שֶׁבַּשָּׁמַיִם וּבָאָרֶץ.

שִׁבְעָה מִי יוֹדֵעַ? שִׁבְעָה אֲנִי יוֹדֵעַ: שִׁבְעָה יְמֵי שַׁבַּתָּא, שִׁשָּׁה סִדְרֵי מִשְׁנָה, חֲמִשָּׁה חוּמְשֵׁי תוֹרָה, אַרְבַּע אִמָּהוֹת, שְׁלֹשָׁה אָבוֹת, שְׁנֵי לֻחוֹת הַבְּרִית, אֶחָד אֱלֹהֵינוּ שֶׁבַּשָּׁמַיִם וּבָאָרֶץ.

שְׁמוֹנָה מִי יוֹדֵעַ? שְׁמוֹנָה אֲנִי יוֹדֵעַ: שְׁמוֹנָה יְמֵי מִילָה, שִׁבְעָה יְמֵי שַׁבַּתָּא, שִׁשָּׁה סִדְרֵי מִשְׁנָה, חֲמִשָּׁה חוּמְשֵׁי תוֹרָה, אַרְבַּע אִמָּהוֹת, שְׁלֹשָׁה אָבוֹת, שְׁנֵי לֻחוֹת הַבְּרִית, אֶחָד אֱלֹהֵינוּ שֶׁבַּשָּׁמַיִם וּבָאָרֶץ.

תִּשְׁעָה מִי יוֹדֵעַ? תִּשְׁעָה אֲנִי יוֹדֵעַ: תִּשְׁעָה יַרְחֵי לֵדָה, שְׁמוֹנָה יְמֵי מִילָה, שִׁבְעָה יְמֵי שַׁבַּתָּא, שִׁשָּׁה סִדְרֵי מִשְׁנָה, חֲמִשָּׁה חוּמְשֵׁי תוֹרָה, אַרְבַּע אִמָּהוֹת, שְׁלֹשָׁה אָבוֹת, שְׁנֵי לֻחוֹת הַבְּרִית, אֶחָד אֱלֹהֵינוּ שֶׁבַּשָּׁמַיִם וּבָאָרֶץ.

עֲשָׂרָה מִי יוֹדֵעַ? עֲשָׂרָה אֲנִי יוֹדֵעַ: עֲשָׂרָה דִבְּרַיָּא, תִּשְׁעָה יַרְחֵי לֵדָה, שְׁמוֹנָה יְמֵי מִילָה, שִׁבְעָה יְמֵי שַׁבַּתָּא, שִׁשָּׁה סִדְרֵי מִשְׁנָה, חֲמִשָּׁה חוּמְשֵׁי תוֹרָה, אַרְבַּע אִמָּהוֹת, שְׁלֹשָׁה אָבוֹת, שְׁנֵי לֻחוֹת הַבְּרִית, אֶחָד אֱלֹהֵינוּ שֶׁבַּשָּׁמַיִם וּבָאָרֶץ.

אֶחָד עָשָׂר מִי יוֹדֵעַ? אֶחָד עָשָׂר אֲנִי יוֹדֵעַ: אֶחָד עָשָׂר כּוֹכְבַיָּא, עֲשָׂרָה דִּבְּרַיָּא,
תִּשְׁעָה יַרְחֵי לֵדָה, שְׁמוֹנָה יְמֵי מִילָה, שִׁבְעָה יְמֵי שַׁבַּתָּא, שִׁשָּׁה סִדְרֵי מִשְׁנָה,
חֲמִשָּׁה חוּמְשֵׁי תוֹרָה, אַרְבַּע אִמָּהוֹת, שְׁלֹשָׁה אָבוֹת, שְׁנֵי לֻחוֹת הַבְּרִית, אֶחָד
אֱלֹהֵינוּ שֶׁבַּשָּׁמַיִם וּבָאָרֶץ.

שְׁנֵים עָשָׂר מִי יוֹדֵעַ? שְׁנֵים עָשָׂר אֲנִי יוֹדֵעַ: שְׁנֵים עָשָׂר שִׁבְטַיָּא, אֶחָד עָשָׂר
כּוֹכְבַיָּא, עֲשָׂרָה דִּבְּרַיָּא, תִּשְׁעָה יַרְחֵי לֵדָה, שְׁמוֹנָה יְמֵי מִילָה, שִׁבְעָה יְמֵי
שַׁבַּתָּא, שִׁשָּׁה סִדְרֵי מִשְׁנָה, חֲמִשָּׁה חוּמְשֵׁי תוֹרָה, אַרְבַּע אִמָּהוֹת, שְׁלֹשָׁה אָבוֹת,
שְׁנֵי לֻחוֹת הַבְּרִית, אֶחָד אֱלֹהֵינוּ שֶׁבַּשָּׁמַיִם וּבָאָרֶץ.

שְׁלֹשָׁה עָשָׂר מִי יוֹדֵעַ? שְׁלֹשָׁה עָשָׂר אֲנִי יוֹדֵעַ: שְׁלֹשָׁה עָשָׂר מִדַּיָּא. שְׁנֵים
עָשָׂר שִׁבְטַיָּא, אֶחָד עָשָׂר כּוֹכְבַיָּא, עֲשָׂרָה דִּבְּרַיָּא, תִּשְׁעָה יַרְחֵי לֵדָה, שְׁמוֹנָה
יְמֵי מִילָה, שִׁבְעָה יְמֵי שַׁבַּתָּא, שִׁשָּׁה סִדְרֵי מִשְׁנָה, חֲמִשָּׁה חוּמְשֵׁי תוֹרָה, אַרְבַּע
אִמָּהוֹת, שְׁלֹשָׁה אָבוֹת, שְׁנֵי לֻחוֹת הַבְּרִית, אֶחָד אֱלֹהֵינוּ שֶׁבַּשָּׁמַיִם וּבָאָרֶץ.

Who knows one? I know one: One is our God in the heavens and the earth.

Who knows two? I know two: two are the tablets of the covenant, One is our God in the heavens and the earth.

Who knows three? I know three: three are the fathers, two are the tablets of the covenant, One is our God in the heavens and the earth.

Who knows four? I know four: four are the mothers, three are the fathers, two are the tablets of the covenant, One is our God in the heavens and the earth.

Who knows five? I know five: five are the books of the Torah, four are the mothers, three are the fathers, two are the tablets of the covenant, One is our God in the heavens and the earth.

Who knows six? I know six: six are the orders of the Mishnah, five are the books of the Torah, four are the mothers, three are the fathers, two are the tablets of the covenant, One is our God in the heavens and the earth.

Who knows seven? I know seven: seven are the days of the week, six are the orders of the Mishnah, five are the books of the Torah, four are the mothers, three are the fathers, two are the tablets of the covenant, One is our God in the heavens and the earth.

Who knows eight? I know eight: eight are the days of circumcision, seven are the days of the week, six are the orders of the Mishnah, five are the books of the Torah, four are the mothers, three are the fathers, two are the tablets of the covenant, One is our God in the heavens and the earth.

Who knows nine? I know nine: nine are the months of birth, eight are the days of circumcision, seven are the days of the week, six are the orders of the Mishnah, five are the books of the Torah, four are the mothers, three are the fathers, two are the tablets of the covenant, One is our God in the heavens and the earth.

Who knows ten? I know ten: ten are the statements, nine are the months of birth, eight are the days of circumcision, seven are the days of the week, six are the orders of the Mishnah, five are the books of the Torah, four are the mothers, three are the fathers, two are the tablets of the covenant, One is our God in the heavens and the earth.

Who knows eleven? I know eleven: eleven are the stars, ten are the statements, nine are the months of birth, eight are the days of circumcision, seven are the days of the week, six are the orders of the Mishnah, five are the books of the Torah, four are the mothers, three are the fathers, two are the tablets of the covenant, One is our God in the heavens and the earth.

Who knows twelve? I know twelve: twelve are the tribes, eleven are the stars, ten are the statements, nine are the months of birth, eight are the days of circumcision, seven are the days of the week, six are the orders of the Mishnah, five are the books of the Torah, four are the mothers, three are the fathers, two are the tablets of the covenant, One is our God in the heavens and the earth.

Who knows thirteen? I know thirteen: thirteen are [God's] attributes, twelve are the tribes, eleven are the stars, ten are the statements, nine are the months of birth, eight are the days of circumcision, seven are the days of the week, six are the orders of the Mishnah, five are the books of the Torah, four are the mothers, three are the fathers, two are the tablets of the covenant, One is our God in the heavens and the earth.

חַד גַּדְיָא
Chad Gadya
One Kid Goat

The final song of the Seder, Chad Gadya, One Kid Goat, is mysterious in a number of ways. It has nothing to do with Passover, and we neither know when it was written nor who wrote it. But it is clearly an allegory about life in general and about the Jewish people in particular. The Jewish people is the goat described in the first verse, and it is subsequently devoured by all animals, people, and natural phenomena—until, at the end, God vanquishes it.

Rabbi Shmuel Goldin writes: "By weaving a tale in which seemingly random violence ultimately gives way to God's will, this *piyut* [poem] urges us not to be misled by 'appearances' around us. God is present in our world, Chad Gadya declares, even when He is hidden; our lives are not governed by chance but by divine plans beyond our comprehension. We are travelling toward a day when all will become clear."

חַד גַּדְיָא, חַד גַּדְיָא דְּזַבִּין אַבָּא בִּתְרֵי זוּזֵי, חַד גַּדְיָא, חַד גַּדְיָא.

וְאָתָא שׁוּנְרָא וְאָכְלָה לְגַדְיָא, דְּזַבִּין אַבָּא בִּתְרֵי זוּזֵי. חַד גַּדְיָא, חַד גַּדְיָא.

וְאָתָא כַלְבָּא וְנָשַׁךְ לְשׁוּנְרָא, דְּאָכְלָה לְגַדְיָא, דְּזַבִּין אַבָּא בִּתְרֵי זוּזֵי. חַד גַּדְיָא, חַד גַּדְיָא.

וְאָתָא חוּטְרָא וְהִכָּה לְכַלְבָּא, דְּנָשַׁךְ לְשׁוּנְרָא, דְּאָכְלָה לְגַדְיָא, דְּזַבִּין אַבָּא בִּתְרֵי זוּזֵי. חַד גַּדְיָא, חַד גַּדְיָא.

וְאָתָא נוּרָא וְשָׂרַף לְחוּטְרָא, דְּהִכָּה לְכַלְבָּא, דְּנָשַׁךְ לְשׁוּנְרָא, דְּאָכְלָה לְגַדְיָא, דְּזַבִּין אַבָּא בִּתְרֵי זוּזֵי. חַד גַּדְיָא, חַד גַּדְיָא.

וְאָתָא מַיָּא וְכָבָה לְנוּרָא, דְּשָׂרַף לְחוּטְרָא, דְּהִכָּה לְכַלְבָּא, דְּנָשַׁךְ לְשׁוּנְרָא, דְּאָכְלָה לְגַדְיָא, דְּזַבִּין אַבָּא בִּתְרֵי זוּזֵי. חַד גַּדְיָא, חַד גַּדְיָא.

וְאָתָא תוֹרָא וְשָׁתָה לְמַיָּא, דְּכָבָה לְנוּרָא, דְּשָׂרַף לְחוּטְרָא, דְּהִכָּה לְכַלְבָּא, דְּנָשַׁךְ לְשׁוּנְרָא, דְּאָכְלָה לְגַדְיָא, דְּזַבִּין אַבָּא בִּתְרֵי זוּזֵי. חַד גַּדְיָא, חַד גַּדְיָא.

וְאָתָא הַשּׁוֹחֵט וְשָׁחַט לְתוֹרָא, דְּשָׁתָה לְמַיָּא, דְּכָבָה לְנוּרָא, דְּשָׂרַף לְחוּטְרָא, דְּהִכָּה לְכַלְבָּא, דְּנָשַׁךְ לְשׁוּנְרָא, דְּאָכְלָה לְגַדְיָא, דְּזַבִּין אַבָּא בִּתְרֵי זוּזֵי. חַד גַּדְיָא, חַד גַּדְיָא.

וְאָתָא מַלְאָךְ הַמָּוֶת וְשָׁחַט לְשׁוֹחֵט, דְּשָׁחַט לְתוֹרָא, דְּשָׁתָה לְמַיָּא, דְּכָבָה לְנוּרָא, דְּשָׂרַף לְחוּטְרָא, דְּהִכָּה לְכַלְבָּא, דְּנָשַׁךְ לְשׁוּנְרָא, דְּאָכְלָה לְגַדְיָא, דְּזַבִּין אַבָּא בִּתְרֵי זוּזֵי. חַד גַּדְיָא, חַד גַּדְיָא.

וְאָתָא הַקָּדוֹשׁ בָּרוּךְ הוּא וְשָׁחַט לְמַלְאַךְ הַמָּוֶת, דְּשָׁחַט לְשׁוֹחֵט, דְּשָׁחַט לְתוֹרָא,
דְּשָׁתָה לְמַיָּא, דְּכָבָה לְנוּרָא, דְּשָׂרַף לְחוּטְרָא, דְּהִכָּה לְכַלְבָּא, דְּנָשַׁךְ לְשׁוּנְרָא,
דְּאָכְלָה לְגַדְיָא, דְּזַבִּין אַבָּא בִּתְרֵי זוּזֵי. חַד גַּדְיָא, חַד גַּדְיָא.

One kid, one kid that my father bought for two zuz, one kid, one kid.

Then came a cat and ate the kid that my father bought for two zuz, one kid, one kid.

Then came a dog and bit the cat, that ate the kid that my father bought for two zuz, one kid, one kid.

Then came a stick and hit the dog, that bit the cat, that ate the kid that my father bought for two zuz, one kid, one kid.

Then came fire and burnt the stick, that hit the dog, that bit the cat, that ate the kid that my father bought for two zuz, one kid, one kid.

Then came water and extinguished the fire, that burnt the stick, that hit the dog, that bit the cat, that ate the kid that my father bought for two zuz, one kid, one kid.

Then came a bull and drank the water, that extinguished the fire, that burnt the stick, that hit the dog, that bit the cat, that ate the kid that my father bought for two zuz, one kid, one kid.

Then came the shochet [ritual slaughterer] and slaughtered the bull, that drank the water, that extinguished the fire, that burnt the stick, that hit the dog, that bit the cat, that ate the kid that my father bought for two zuz, one kid, one kid.

Then came the angel of death and slaughtered the shochet, who slaughtered the bull, that drank the water, that extinguished the fire, that burnt the stick, that hit the dog, that bit the cat, that ate the kid that my father bought for two zuz, one kid, one kid.

Then came the Holy One, blessed be He, and slaughtered the angel of death, who slaughtered the shochet, who slaughtered the bull, that drank the water, that extinguished the fire, that burnt the stick, that hit the dog, that bit the cat, that ate the kid that my father bought for two zuz, one kid, one kid.

The Principles of the Jewish Faith

If you've ever wondered what Judaism is, here is a list of its principal beliefs. This is not an official list, but each of these beliefs is held by religious Jews. It is included in this Haggadah because fewer and fewer Jews—and few non-Jews—know much about Judaism. And because it will provoke much discussion at your Seder table.

I. There is one universal God.
This God is the Creator of the world and the God of all humanity.

II. One universal God means there is one universal morality.

III. God is:
　　a) Incorporeal (not physical): All matter comes to an end.
　　b) Eternal: All matter had a beginning and will have an end. But God exists outside of time.
　　c) Outside of nature: God is not in nature. And nature is not divine.
　　d) Personal: God knows each of us.
　　e) Good: God is moral, just, and compassionate.

IV. God is the God revealed in the Torah—the God of Creation, the God of Israel, the God of the Ten Commandments.

V. God's primary demand is that people be good.
Therefore:
　　a) God cares most about how humans act toward one another.
　　b) Right behavior matters more than right intentions and even more than right faith.

VI. There is an afterlife—God rewards the good and punishes the bad.
If good people and bad people have the same fate, there is either no God or God is not just.

VII. Though there is an afterlife, God wants us to be preoccupied with this life.

VIII. Reward in the afterlife ("heaven") is available to all good people, not just good Jews.

IX. Human beings are not born basically good.

a) Therefore, evil comes primarily from within the human being, not from external causes such as poverty. (One proof of the latter is that there is no shortage of bad people who are wealthy.)

b) Therefore, the most important task of society must be to make good people, which is Judaism's primary task.

X. All people are created in the image of God.

a) Therefore, racism is theologically untenable.

b) Therefore, the most important distinction among human beings is not their race, religion, nationality, class or sex; it is their behavior. In the words of Viktor Frankl, psychiatrist and Holocaust survivor, "There are only two races, the decent and the indecent."

c) Therefore, human life is sacred and animal life is not (though we are forbidden to inflict gratuitous suffering on animals).

XI. God created the world for man.

Therefore, there is no purpose to nature without man to appreciate and (responsibly) use it.

XII. The Jews are the Chosen People, chosen to bring mankind to the God of the Torah and to the Ten Commandments (but not necessarily to Judaism).

Chosenness has therefore never meant that the Jews are better than anyone else. Indeed, the Torah, and the entire Hebrew Bible, goes out of its way to depict the Jews as flawed, just like everyone else.

XIII. The Torah is from God.

This does not mean that only a literal reading of the Torah is valid. It means that the Torah ultimately comes from God, not men.

XIV. Judaism is comprised of God, Torah, and Israel (meaning both Jewish peoplehood and the Land of Israel).

The removal of any one of them is no longer Judaism.

XV. Jewish faith rests on two pillars: Creation and Exodus.
Both are divine events.

XVI. Judaism is a religion of distinctions.
Among these distinctions are: a) God and man, b) good and evil, c) man and woman, d) holy and profane, e) parent and child, f) God and nature, g) human and animal, h) life and death.

XVII. Judaism can ennoble anyone.
Therefore, anyone is welcome to embrace Judaism and become a member of the Jewish people. No one is obligated to become a Jew, but everyone is obligated to be good.

Notes

1. The Rabbis developed an elaborate system to ensure that Passover always falls in the spring. Had the holiday followed the 354-day lunar calendar, the calendar by which Judaism operates, it would fall at different times in different years just as the Muslim month of Ramadan does. (For example, every six years Passover would fall some sixty-six days earlier than the time originally ordained for the holiday's observance.) The Rabbis added a month to the Hebrew calendar seven out of every nineteen years to ensure, in keeping with Deuteronomy 16:1, that Passover remain a spring holiday. The extra month is the month that precedes Passover to ensure Passover doesn't fall too early.

2. Mishnah *Pesachim* 10:1.

3. Walter Kaufmann, *Religions in Four Dimensions* (New York: Reader's Digest Press, 1976).

4. Justin P. McBrayer, associate professor of philosophy at Fort Lewis College in Durango, Colorado, "Why Our Children Don't Think There Are Moral Facts," *New York Times*, March 2, 2015, https://opinionator.blogs.nytimes.com/2015/03/02/why-our-children-dont-think-there-are-moral-facts/.

5. Written in a letter cited by Hugh S. Moorhead, *The Meaning of Life* (Chicago: Chicago Review Press, 1988). The letter may be viewed here: https://archive.org/details/meaningoflifeoohugh/page/164/mode/2up.

6. Jonathan Sacks, "Passover Tells Us: Teach Your Children Well," The Office of Rabbi Sacks, April 17, 2011, https://rabbisacks.org/passover-tells-us-teach-your-children-well-published-in-the-huffington-post/.

7. Mishnah *Pesachim* 10:8.

8. Exodus 13:8.

9. A number of reasons are offered in *The Rational Bible* commentary on Exodus 1:15 and 18.

10. Talmud *Shavuot* 29a.

11. Erich Fromm, *You Shall Be as Gods: A Radical Interpretation of the Old Testament* (New York: Henry Holt and Company, 1966).

12. Each is explained at length in the commentary on the Second Commandment in *The Rational Bible* commentary on Exodus and Deuteronomy.

13. Peter Merkl, *Political Violence under the Swastika* (Princeton, New Jersey: Princeton University Press, 1975).

14. George Watson, *The Economist*, December 1973.

15. Jay P. Greene et al., "Are Educated People More Anti-Semitic?" Tablet, March 29, 2021, https://www.tabletmag.com/sections/news/articles/are-educated-people -more-anti-semitic-jay-greene-albert-cheng-ian-kingsbury.

16. Jerusalem Talmud, *Kiddushin* 4:12.

17. "From John Adams to Massachusetts Militia, October 11, 1798," Founders Online, National Archives, https://founders.archives.gov/documents/Adams/99-02-02-3102.

18. *The Federalist Papers* no. 55.

19. *Midrash Rabba Bamidbar* 20:11.

Selected Essays from
The Rational Bible: Exodus

The following essays—five on God and one on ritual—are taken from *The Rational Bible*, my five-volume commentary on the Torah. They are appended to this Haggadah because of the centrality of God to the Exodus (that is the reason Moses is not mentioned in the Haggadah) and, of course, to meaning and morality; and because of the centrality of ritual to Judaism. The purpose of *The Rational Bible* is to explain the Torah, the most important book in history, to modern men and women. I regard ignorance of the Torah and the rest of the Bible as the single most important reason for the present existential crisis of Western civilization.

Essay: Belief in God is a Choice—and Why to Make It

3.3 Moses said, "I must turn aside to look at this marvelous sight; why doesn't the bush burn up?"

One can assume just about anyone who keeps looking at a burning bush will eventually wonder why the fire isn't burning the bush and what is sustaining the fire. But it is also true most people would not keep looking. After a first glance, and the realization the fire seemed contained, there would be nothing to prompt most people to continue to look. But Moses did continue looking and he noticed something unique, even miraculous, was taking place.

If you wait for God to contact you before you lead a God-centered life, you will almost surely never lead a life with God in it.

In a sense, Moses's behavior exemplifies a choice we all have when looking at life—am I seeing a miracle? Is the birth of a baby a miracle? Is thought, consciousness, great art—and, for that matter, all existence—a miracle? That is our choice to make.

The Victorian-era British poet, Elizabeth Barrett Browning, commented on this verse:

> Earth's crammed with heaven,
> And every common bush afire with God
> But only he who sees takes off his shoes....

"Only he who sees..."

That's the great question: Who sees the miracles of daily life?

And the answer is: Whoever chooses to see.

One of the most important lessons of life—one I believe most people never learn—is that almost everything important is a choice. We choose whether to be happy (or, at the very least whether to act happy), whether to be a hard worker, whether to be honest, whether to be kind, whether to see miracles, and, yes, whether to believe in God (or, at the very least, live as if there is a God).

At an early age, I decided to believe in God and lead a God-centered and religious life. I was well aware of all the arguments against belief in God. And God never directly appeared to me.

I made this decision because:

1. I came to realize the terrible consequences of a world without God.

•   If there is no God, life is ultimately pointless—the product of mere random chance. We humans therefore have no more ultimate meaning than rocks. Just as rocks came about by chance, will eventually cease to exist, and leave behind no record of their existence, if there is no God, the same holds true for every one of us—we, too, came about by chance, will cease to exist (much sooner than rocks), and leave behind no lasting record of our existence. (How many of our ancestors can we name, let alone know anything about? Start with any of your sixteen great-great-grandparents.)

A secular scholar of Greek philosophy writing in the *New York Times* perfectly captured this view:

"Eventually everything ends in heat death. The universe certainly started with a bang, but it likely ends with a fizzle.

What's the purpose in that, though?

There isn't one. The universe as we understand it tells us nothing about the goal or meaning of existence, let alone our own. In the grand scheme of things, you and I are enormously insignificant.

I will never see my Papa again. One day I will die. So will you. [We] will decay along with everything in the universe as the fundamental particles we're made of return to the inert state in which everything began."

Since I do not believe existence in general and human life in particular are nothing more than a purposeless coalescing of stellar dust, I have to conclude there is a God.

- If there is no God, good and evil do not objectively exist because if there is no God, there is no non-material reality. Only the physical exists, and good and evil are not physical properties; they are moral properties. Therefore, if there is no God, the terms "good" and "evil" are subjective opinions, not objective realities. People and societies call "good" what they approve of, and call "evil" what they disapprove of. To be sure, this does not mean an atheist cannot be a good person or a God-believer cannot be a bad person. It only means the existence of a moral God is necessary for morality to objectively exist. People will counter, "To which God are you referring?" since not all conceptions of God agree on what is good or evil. The answer is the God introduced to the world by this Torah: the God of Creation and of the Ten Commandments. Many people and religions use the word "God," but the "God" about whom they are speaking is not necessarily the original one—the one introduced by this Torah.

  Honest people can debate God's existence. But what is not debatable is the absence of an objective good and evil if there is no God. Atheist philosophers acknowledge this. When I debated the subject, "Can We Be Good without God?" at Oxford University with the eminent British moral philosopher Professor Jonathan Glover, an atheist, one of the first things he said was "...if there isn't a God, there is only subjective morality. That's absolutely true."

The eminent Princeton philosopher Richard Rorty acknowledged that for secular liberals such as himself, "there is no answer to the question, 'Why not be cruel?'"

Therefore, believing good and evil really do exist, I have no logical choice but to believe in a moral God.

- If there is no God, the only reality is material (physical). Only if there is a God (Who is not material) does anything non-material actually exist—including everything we most cherish, such as love and the mind. If there is no God, love is nothing more than the interaction of neurons in the brain or the effects of hormones on the brain. And if there is no God, the "mind" is just the material brain deceiving itself into believing it exists. If only matter is real, the mind is merely another physical part of the brain. Therefore, as I do not believe love is only the interplay of neurons or the effect of hormones, I believe in God. And as I believe there is a mind, not only a physical brain, I believe there is a God.

2. I chose to believe in God because I wanted to lead the deepest, richest, and most hope-filled life possible.

All that is provided only by a God-centered and religion-centered life. Virtually every poll measuring the happiness of people living in the West finds religious individuals are more at peace, happier, live longer, and enjoy a more communal life.

In the words of a study conducted by the Austin Institute for the Study of Family and Culture, "Research has suggested that religious faith may be adept in its ability to offer significance and meaning to life, that religious coping mechanisms can improve physical and emotional health, that faith can be a powerful motivating force, and that congregants may receive emotional support from others in their congregations."

In light of this, the most important question to ask an atheist is this: "Do you hope you are right or wrong?"

Virtually every atheist I have debated (and I have debated many) has said that while they cannot, for intellectual (and emotional) reasons, believe in God, they certainly would wish God did exist. How could they not? Who wouldn't want to believe life has ultimate meaning, good and evil really exist, the good are rewarded and the evil punished, death doesn't end everything, and we will be reunited with those we love?

> *You can be an agnostic intellectually. But you cannot live as an agnostic. You live as either a believer or as an atheist.*

It is a deeper life to begin each meal with a blessing.

It is a deeper life to have a community to which you are attached and which cares about you. In theory, such secular communities can exist, but they rarely do.

It is a deeper life to gather with people and study holy texts such as the Torah. Of course, secular people can gather and regularly study, let us say, Shakespeare. But for every Shakespeare study group, there are probably a thousand Bible study groups.

It is a deeper life to have a weekly Sabbath, during which normal work ceases and one spends hours with loved ones and/or members of one's religious community.

Therefore, deeply wanting to live such a richer life, I chose to believe in God.

3. I want to live with hope.

This world is saturated with injustice. Enormous numbers of good people suffer horribly, and a great number of unjust people are never brought to justice. Only if the just God of the Torah exists can there be ultimate justice. Only if this God exists, do the good receive their just rewards and the evil receive their just punishments. That, of course, can only happen if there is an afterlife (the existence of which is discussed on a number of occasions in this commentary). And only if there is a God is there an afterlife—the only hope that death doesn't end our existence, and that of everyone we love.

Therefore, as I want to live with hope, I have chosen to believe in God.

Of course, there are those who dismiss such a choice as mere wishful thinking.

I readily admit I wish there is a good God, ultimate justice, an afterlife, and meaning to my life. Every normal person wishes the same. But that does not make belief in God solely a product of wishful thinking. I believe in God for a host of rational reasons, one of which is the unique greatness of the Torah and the Bible. Moreover, all those atheists who believe there is (or, more precisely, who manufacture) some ultimate purpose to their lives should recognize their entire philosophy of a meaningful life really is based on wishful thinking—precisely what they accuse believers of.

Moreover, while I readily admit that for all these reasons I made the choice to believe in God, these are not the only reasons. The arguments for God's existence are far more rationally powerful than the atheist argument that everything—life, intelligence, consciousness, the entire universe—came about by itself.

> "*All of our observations find a complete symmetry between matter and antimatter, which is why the universe should not actually exist.*"
>
> **—CERN, the European Organization for Nuclear Research**

Science would seem to confirm the miracle of life. The more science reveals about the brain, the further it is from understanding how it operates; the inability of science to explain the development of life from non-life (the organic from the inorganic); the immeasurable odds against intelligent life existing; or the latest insoluble puzzle, as revealed by CERN, the European Organization for Nuclear Research:

All of our observations find a complete symmetry between matter and antimatter, which is why *the universe should not actually exist.*

So, again, I acknowledge that belief in God—or in atheism—is indeed a choice. But as noted at the beginning of this essay, virtually everything worthwhile is a choice. Love is a choice, leading a good life is a choice, marriage is a choice, (for most people) having children is a choice, working hard is a choice, taking care of others is a choice, learning a musical instrument or a foreign language instead of playing video games is a choice.

I see no good reason not to make this choice—and myriad reasons to do so.

Yet, while an ever-increasing number of people consider themselves agnostic, the great majority of these people *live* as if they are atheists, bereft of all the magnificent life-enhancing benefits a God-centered life provides. These individuals are agnostics intellectually, but atheists behaviorally.

Such people need to make a choice: Will I live as if there is a God or as if there is no God? You can be an agnostic intellectually, but you cannot *live* as an agnostic; you live as either a believer or as an atheist. You live either as if life is random chance or as if it is infused with ultimate meaning.

Moses *chose* to look carefully and see a miracle in that burning bush. If we look carefully, we, too, will see a miracle—in everything.

ESSAY: THE GOD OF THE TORAH: THE MOST IMPORTANT IDEA IN WORLD HISTORY

1. The God introduced by the Torah is the first god in history to have been entirely above and beyond nature. And one of the first things God tells humans is to exercise dominion over nature (Genesis 1:26-28). This liberated humanity from believing it was controlled by nature, a revolution that made moral and scientific progress possible.

A second consequence of God being above nature is humans are not part of nature—meaning that just as we are to control the natural world outside us, we are to control our own human nature within us as well. We are to govern our lives by moral law, not by human nature.

2. The God introduced by the Torah brought universal morality into the world. Only if a moral God is universal, is morality universal. Morality was no longer local or individual. Cultures do not need to be universal; the world is enriched by multiple cultures. But morality must be universal.

3. The moral God introduced by the Torah means morality is real. "Good" and "evil" are not merely individual or societal opinions, but objectively real.

4. The God introduced by the Torah morally judges every human being. There had never been a concept like this. And it became a major reason for Jew-hatred. People do not like to be judged, and the people who introduced the idea of a God who morally judges people have paid a terrible price for bringing the idea into the world. The social psychologist Ernest van den Haag wrote:

> Fundamental to [anti-Semitism] though seldom explicit and conscious is hostility to the Jewish belief in one God.... [The Jews'] invisible God not only insisted on being the one and only and all-powerful God—creator and lord of everything, and the only rightful claimant to worship—He also developed into a moral God.... No wonder [the Jews] are the target of all those who resent His domination.

Having dialogued with atheists for decades, I have come to believe at least some of the current aggressive atheism is due to an animosity toward the idea there is a God Who will judge all of us (another reason is all the evil done in the name of God by radical Islamists—the worst sin according to the Ten Commandments [see Commandment 3 in Exodus 20]).

5. The just and good God introduced by the Torah gives humanity hope. One of those hopes is there is ultimate justice. The belief that God judges humans means both the good and the evil will get what they ultimately deserve. Even though justice is rarely served in this world, there is a good God who will ultimately set things right.

6. The God introduced by the Torah introduced holiness—the elevation of human beings from animals to creatures created in the divine image (see commentary to Leviticus 19:2).

7. The God introduced by the Torah gives every individual unprecedented self-worth. Since all humans are created in God's image, each of us is infinitely valuable. Every person has the right to say, as the Talmud put it, "For my sake was the world created."

The nineteenth-century Hasidic master Rabbi Simcha Bunim suggested that every person carry in his or her pockets two pieces of paper. On one should be written, "For my sake was the world created," while the other should contain the words "I am but dust and ashes" (the words Abraham said when he argued with God in Genesis 18:27). Each paper should be consulted at the appropriate time. When you feel arrogant and proud of how much more you have achieved than others, remind yourself you are "but dust and ashes." And when you are feeling despair, remind yourself, "For my sake was the world created." There is some special mission and task only you can accomplish.

8. The God introduced by the Torah is necessary for human brotherhood. Since we all have the same Father, we are all brothers and sisters. As the Prophet Malachi asked: "Have we not all one Father? Did not one God create us?" (Malachi 2:10).

9. The God introduced by the Torah began the long journey to belief in human equality—solely as a result of the Torah statement that each of us is created in God's image. Slavery was abolished on a wide scale first in the

Western world—by Christians who were rooted in the Torah and the rest of the Hebrew Bible and who specifically cited the Torah doctrine that all humans are created in God's image.

10. The God introduced by the Torah is incorporeal (no body; not physical). This opened the human mind to abstract thought by enabling humans to think in terms of a reality beyond that which is accessible to our senses.

11. The God introduced by the Torah teaches us the physical is not the only reality. Consequently, there can be non-physical realities such as a soul, an afterlife, and morality.

12. The God introduced by the Torah means there is ultimate meaning to existence and to each of our lives. Without this Creator, existence is random and purposeless.

That people make up meanings for their lives is a fine thing (at least, when that meaning is moral; many things—evil ideologies are the most obvious example—that give people meaning are not moral), but these meanings are nothing more than artificial constructs.

As one atheist professor expressed it, in summarizing the work of another atheist philosopher:

> Ultimately, our lives are meaningless. Evolution is blind and serves no intrinsic purpose; in a cosmic sense, we each live for an insignificant amount of time....
>
> [David] Benatar, a professor of philosophy at the University of Cape Town, argues that humans can enjoy "terrestrial" meanings—nurturing children, fighting for the rights of refugees, composing a symphony or making a delicious breakfast, for example.... Nevertheless, we are each but a "blip in cosmic time and space." Mr. Benatar insists that most of us are terminally anxious about this lack of cosmic meaning....
>
> I did a very unscientific poll of my friends. None of them believe that there is some wider purpose to human existence.

13. The God introduced by the Torah gives human beings free will. If we are only material beings (like the stellar dust of which we are composed), everything we do is determined by our genes and by our environment. Only if we have a non-material soul can we rise above our genes and our environment and act autonomously. The secular denial of anything beyond the physical deprives human beings of free will. That is why Clarence Darrow, the most famous criminal defense lawyer in American history (as well as America's most famous religious skeptic), opposed all punishment of criminals: "All people are products of two things, and two things only—their heredity and environment. And they act in exact accord with the heredity which they took from all the past and for which they are in no wise responsible, and the environment."

> *The just and good God introduced by the Torah gave humanity hope that there is ultimate justice.*

14. The God introduced by the Torah teaches might is not right. It is God Who determines what is right, not displays of strength and force.

15. Finally, the God introduced by the Torah made human moral progress possible. Indeed, the Torah invented human moral progress. In the words of New York University historian Henry Bamford Parkes, "Judaism [starting with the Torah] repudiated the cyclic view of history *held by all other ancient peoples* and affirmed that it was a meaningful process leading to the gradual regeneration of humanity. *This was the origin of the Western belief in progress...*" (emphases added).

What was "the cyclic view of history" referred to by Professor Parkes? In ancient civilizations, life was a cycle, meaning nothing changed from generation to generation. Every generation essentially repeated what came before it. There was therefore no such thing as moral progress—indeed, the word "progress" would have been meaningless. Then came the Torah and its God, and life was no longer to be a cycle, but a line—a line moving forward toward a moral goal.

ESSAY: THE DIFFERENCE BETWEEN BELIEF IN GOD AND FAITH IN GOD

4.23 (cont.) Now I will slay your first-born son.'"

Few readers, even veteran students of the Bible, recall the killing of Pharaoh's firstborn son, which transpired during the tenth plague, was mentioned by God to Moses even before the plagues began. But Moses does not repeat those words to Pharaoh at this point. Perhaps he feared it would provoke Pharaoh to kill him.

If that is indeed the reason Moses does not fulfill this explicit order from God, it would reveal that, at that point, he lacked complete faith God would protect him. He would come to faith later; but at this point, both God and His promises were quite new to Moses. In a sense, then, one could say even God has to establish credibility to be fully trusted.

Which raises the issue of trust, or faith, in God.

There are two distinct meanings to the statement, "I believe in God."

The first meaning is, "I believe God exists."

The second meaning is, "I trust in God."

The first is the most common meaning, but it is not nearly as important as the second. To believe God exists but not have trust, or faith, in Him is the same as believing another person exists but not having trust in that person.

The importance of trust in God has been so fundamental to American history, for example, that one of the two mottos of the United States since the nineteenth century has been, "In God We Trust" (the other is *e pluribus unum*—Latin for "from many, one"). The motto's words were carefully chosen; they were not "We Believe in God."

So, then, what does trust, or faith, in God mean?

Does it mean, as many people assume, trusting God will help us whenever we are in trouble? Clearly, that cannot be the case. An innumerable number of people who have trusted in God have not been helped—certainly not in any direct way—by God when they were in trouble. If God always intervened as we wished, there would be no unjust suffering in this world—no disease, no evil, and no death (and, one should add, no free will). But, of course, there is an immeasurable amount of unjust suffering: If pain were water, the world would drown.

Therefore, trust in God must mean, first and foremost, that we believe God cares about each one of us and in some way He will ultimately do right by us. And that in turn means—in the final analysis—since injustice often prevails in this world, there must be an afterlife, a life in which a just God makes sure justice prevails.

> *To believe God exists but not have trust, or faith, in Him is the same as believing another person exists but not having trust in that person.*

But trust in God also means more than belief in an afterlife. Believers also trust that God will, at times of His choosing, intervene in this world, though not necessarily in the lifetime of any specific individual who might beseech God's intervention. For example, Jews have trusted for thousands of years that God would ensure the Jews would one day return to their homeland—and they did. And, of course, such trust does not only apply to Jews. Many people, myself included, believe God intervened in some way to inspire the founding of the United States of America, a country founded by Christians rooted in the Hebrew Bible. It is not surprising, therefore, that the only verse inscribed on the most iconic symbol of the American Revolution, the Liberty Bell, is from the Torah: "You shall proclaim liberty throughout the land for all its inhabitants" (Leviticus 25:10). America became the one truly Judeo-Christian country.

ESSAY: DO ALL BELIEVERS IN ONE GOD BELIEVE IN THE SAME GOD?

This affirmation of God as the only God—the central theological tenet of the Torah—raises a vitally important question: Do all people who believe in one god believe in the same god? More specifically, do they all believe in this God the Torah introduced to the world?

The answer—and to many this may come as a surprise—is, no.

The reason this is so important is the God of the Torah (and the rest of the Bible) is often blamed by anti-religious people for any terrible actions committed by anyone who claims to believe in God.

When Jews, Christians, and Muslims—let alone people who identify with no specific religion—say, "I believe in God," they are not necessarily talking about the same God, and certainly not necessarily talking about the God of the Torah. In fact, the statement, "I believe in God," tells us nothing about a person's beliefs or about the god in whom he or she believes.

To cite an obvious example, a god in whose name believers cut innocent people's throats, behead them, burn them alive, and rape girls and women—as is being done at the time of this writing by Islamist terrorists in the name of "the one God"—cannot be the same god as the God of the Torah, the God who gave the Ten Commandments, who commanded His people to "Love the stranger," and demanded holy and ethical conduct at all times. Likewise, those Christians who in the Middle Ages slaughtered entire Jewish communities in the name of Christ also clearly did not believe in the God of the Bible (let alone in those Church leaders who condemned such atrocities)—as virtually every Christian today would acknowledge.

Yet, there are many people who argue that all those who say they believe in God believe in the same God.

Why do people make this argument? Because all too often they have an anti-religious agenda. They say all those who claim to believe in God believe in the same God in order to discredit God and religion, especially religions rooted in the Bible.

So, then, how are we to know whether any two people who say they believe in God believe in the same God, specifically the God of the Torah?

We can find out by asking three questions:

1. *Do you believe in the God known as the "God of Israel"?*

Before responding, some people might need to have the term defined. The "God of Israel" is the God introduced to the world by the Jews and their Bible. This is the God Who created the world, Who revealed Himself to the Jews, and Who made His moral will known through the Ten Commandments and the Hebrew prophets. Obviously, all believing Jews would answer in the affirmative. The great majority of religious Christians would as well.

If, after having "God of Israel" defined, a person cannot answer the question in the affirmative, it is fair to say the individual does not believe in the God of the Torah. He or she believes in another god.

2. *Does the god you believe in judge the moral behavior of every human being—and by the same moral standard?*

There are many people today who say they believe in God, but not in a God who judges people's actions. These people are generally to be found among those who affirm no specific religion. For them, "God" is an entirely personal thing. Often, they will say "God is within me." But, of course, if God is only within them, who outside of them will ever judge them?

> *People who believe in a god who does not morally judge them and all other people do not believe in the God of the Torah.*

They can be fine people. But the question here is not whether there are any good people who do not believe in the God of the Torah. Of course there are. The question is whether all people who say they believe in God believe in the *same* God, and specifically in the God introduced by the Torah.

People who believe in a god who does not morally judge them and all other people do not believe in the God of the Torah. In fact, a god indifferent to the moral behavior of human beings is so different from the God of the Torah that these believers might as well use a word other than "God."

Now, one might argue Islamist terrorists also believe in a judging God, as did Tomas de Torquemada, the infamous Catholic head of the Spanish Inquisition. But this argument is not pertinent, because such individuals believe God judges people by their faith alone, not by their moral behavior—and believers can therefore torture and kill non-believers. That is not the God of the Torah.

It should be clear, but in case it is not, it needs to be emphatically emphasized that one need not be a Jew—or a Christian, or a member of any faith—to believe in the God of the Torah. While it is the Torah's aim that all humanity believe in the God revealed in the Torah, there is not the slightest suggestion anyone needs to become a Jew to do so. Indeed the purpose of the Jewish people—the purpose of being Chosen—is to bring humanity to the God of the Torah, which, by definition, also means accepting God's moral demands (such as the "Noahide Laws" or the Ten Commandments).

The great Benjamin Franklin, one of America's founders, was one such example: He did not affirm the Christian Trinity, and he was not a Jew. But he believed in the God introduced by the Hebrew Bible, in its moral teachings, and that this God morally judges all human beings. As Franklin wrote in his autobiography: "I never doubted, for instance, the existence of the Deity, that he made the world and governed it by his Providence, that the most acceptable service of God was the doing of good to man, that our souls are immortal, and that *all crime will be punished and virtue rewarded either here or hereafter*" (emphasis added).

Franklin and many of America's founders were examples of ethical monotheists. They were the type of people the Torah wants all people to be.

3. *Do you believe in the God who gave the Ten Commandments?*

This question also needs to be asked even though it is included in the first question.

The reason it needs to be asked is if God never revealed His moral will, how would we know what behaviors He demands from us and what acts He judges as wrong?

None of these comments are a judgment of individuals; they are a judgment of the statement, "I believe in God." There are people who do not believe in the God of the Torah, and, for that matter, people who believe in no God, who are fine, upstanding individuals—just as there are people who believe in the God of the Torah who are not decent people. But for reasons made clear throughout this commentary, the best moral hope for mankind is to bring as many people as possible to belief in the God introduced by the Torah, though not necessarily to Judaism or any other religion. (While it is usually best to affiliate with a Torah-based religion, one can believe in the God of the Torah and in the Ten Commandments without being a member of a religion.)

ESSAY: IN RELIGIOUS RITUAL—UNLIKE IN ETHICAL BEHAVIOR—INTENTIONS MATTER

25.2 Tell the Israelite people to bring Me gifts; you shall accept gifts for Me from every person whose heart so moves him.

Ordinarily, the Torah gives commandments we must fulfill regardless of whether our heart is in fulfilling them or not. Moral actions must be taken whether or not our heart prompts us to. Accordingly, the Torah commands that every third year we give ten percent of our earnings to the poor (Deuteronomy 26:12) and an additional percentage each year (Leviticus 19:9-10), irrespective of whether our hearts prompt us to do so. But with regard to giving to God, our hearts can determine how much we give.

Charity is given to people. Therefore it is a moral/ethical act. And regarding the ethical, God does not demand the heart. Good actions—actions that help other human beings—are worthwhile in and of themselves because recipients of charity are helped regardless of our intentions.

Or, to put it another way: Good actions are good, even if animated by selfishness. And bad actions are bad, even if animated by good intentions. If a person builds a hospital because he wants to become famous by having the hospital named for him, that hospital saves just as many lives as hospitals built by people animated solely by altruistic motives. Furthermore, people whose lives are saved by a hospital built by a person who wanted to be famous are just as grateful as those whose lives are saved by hospitals built by selfless people. In ethics, what matters most is results, not intentions.

At the same time, good intentions leading to bad results are worthless. Such is the case, for example, when wealthy nations, for altruistic reasons, give large sums of money to poor countries whose corrupt governments are then strengthened. Such "aid" does more harm than good.

This is also true within wealthier nations. Society must, of course, take care of those who are in real need. But a certain percentage of people who are capable of working and providing for themselves will choose not to work, and instead seek to be financially supported by the government. This in turn leads to three awful consequences:

1. It erodes the character of those relying on such aid.

2. It reduces the amount of resources available to care for the truly needy.

3. It literally makes addicts out of many of these people—they become addicted to receiving unearned income. It can be as difficult to wean people off unearned benefits as it is to wean people off drugs.

Each of these destructive consequences is the product of good intentions.

The history of the modern world is filled with people who have done terrible things from sincere and good motives. The large number of individuals in democracies who supported communist tyrannies is one obvious example.

In other words, *regarding morality, intentions matter little; often, not at all. But when it comes to relating to God (prayer, ritual acts, etc.), intentions matter a great deal.*

The Israelites' gifts will be used to build a place to worship God. This, then, is a ritual act, and when it comes to ritual, our hearts need to be involved if the act is to have significance. Unlike moral actions, which are ends in themselves, *a ritual is not an end in itself* but a means of bringing the individual closer to God and to greater holiness.

God is not restricted to any specific location. This idea about God was another radical innovation of the Torah.

Because all the donations given by the Israelites to building the Tabernacle were voluntary, we come across no grumbling, even though until now the Israelites have repeatedly expressed angry complaints against both God and Moses. That indicates the wisdom of soliciting voluntary contributions in the ritual realm.

Many hundreds of years later, when the Israelites were firmly ensconced in their homeland, King Solomon set out to build the sequel to the Tabernacle, the *Beit Ha-Mikdash*, the Great Temple, in Jerusalem. Solomon, however, chose not to rely on voluntary contributions and imposed forced labor. Ten thousand men were sent each month to work in timber-rich Lebanon, while seventy thousand porters and eighty thousand stonecutters were assigned to labor in Israel. Some 3,300 officials were appointed to oversee the Temple's erection (I Kings 5:27-30).

ESSAY: REASON AND BELIEF

32.4 This he took from them and cast in a mold, and made it into a molten calf. And they exclaimed, "This is your god, O Israel, who brought you out of the land of Egypt!"

It is difficult for us today to believe the people really believed a calf made from molten metals brought them out of Egypt.

First, they already ascribed this to Moses: "that man Moses, who brought us from the land of Egypt..." (verse 1).

Second, they witnessed Aaron fabricate the calf with their own eyes from jewelry they gave him; surely, they had to realize it was not in existence prior to and during their exodus from Egypt.

And third, as Nachmanides writes: "No one in the world could be so stupid as to think that the gold in their ears brought them out of Egypt."

But coming from a pagan culture, one that revered the calf (the sacred bull known as Apis or Hapis was an Egyptian god), they apparently did believe it. The ability of people to suspend reason in order to believe what they want to believe is limitless.

To understand what is wrong here, one must distinguish between the non-rational and the anti-rational (or the "irrational"). There is most certainly a place for the non-rational in life. Much of what is beautiful— love and art, for example—transcends reason. And a great deal of good is achieved by not following the dictates of pure reason. It is not fully rational, for example, to risk one's life to save another person. But there is no place for the *anti*-rational—and ascribing divinity to a molten calf is anti-rational.

Of course, some atheists argue belief in a God Who created the world, acted in history, and revealed His moral will through the Ten Commandments is also contrary to reason. But they equate lack of scientific proof with irrationality. While not scientifically provable, there is nothing anti-rational about believing in a Creator. On the contrary, what is anti-rational is the belief the universe came about by itself, intelligence was not created by intelligence, and life sprang from non-life, even though we have not the slightest evidence it did. Furthermore, there is no comparison between the belief in the Creator God and the God of Exodus and people believing a gold statue just produced from their own jewelry was responsible for freeing them from slavery and leading them out of Egypt.

The latter belief is contrary to reason—a fact that neither troubled the Israelites then nor vast numbers of people today. And one can find belief in the anti-rational in the secular world as well as in the religious world. Think of all the people, especially secular intellectuals, who believed in communism, the ideology that enslaved and murdered more people than any other in history. And think of all the people in Germany and elsewhere who believed in racism, an idea as contrary to reason as belief in a Golden Calf.

> *There is most certainly a place for the non-rational in life. Much of what is beautiful—like love and art—transcends reason. But there is no place for the anti-rational.*

The idea the Israelites, who announced their faith in God and in His servant Moses (Exodus 14:31), suddenly believed a molten calf was the god who took them out of Egypt struck the ancient rabbis as so implausible they held that it emanated from the "mixed multitude" of other oppressed, non-Israelite peoples in Egypt who joined the Exodus (the *erev rav*; see Exodus 12:38). This explanation was not some chauvinistic attempt to avoid blaming the Israelites; the Torah constantly blames the Israelites for their bad conduct. It was based on the language of the verse. The speakers did not say "our god"; they said, "your god," implying they were addressing the Israelites as outsiders.

Bible commentator Professor Jeffrey Tigay notes the "declaration that the calf is the god who brought them out of Egypt contrasted ironically with God's [earlier] declaration that it is through the Tabernacle that He will abide among the Israelites and that *they will know that He is their God who brought them out of Egypt*" (Exodus 29:42-46; emphasis added).

Finally, the verse does not actually say, "This is your god, O Israel." It says, "These are your gods, O Israel." Why the plural, given that only one "god" has been built?

In Cassuto's view, the Israelites regarded "the calf [as] a partner, as it were, of the Lord. Hence the plural." He is probably right. Though strict monotheism characterized biblical thought from the very beginning, it took a long time to become fully and universally rooted among the Israelites. What existed among many ancient Israelites was henotheism—a belief in the one God of Israel, but not *only* in the God of Israel. In other words, the plural sentence implies the Israelites were worshipping the Golden Calf *and* God.